No Boss No Hassle No Plan

Nicc Ravine

Published by New Generation Publishing in 2024

Copyright © Nicc Ravine 2024

First Edition

The author asserts the moral right under the Copyright, Designs and Patents Act 1988 to be identified as the author of this work.

All Rights reserved. No part of this publication may be reproduced, stored in a retrieval system or transmitted, in any form or by any means without the prior consent of the author, nor be otherwise circulated in any form of binding or cover other than that which it is published and without a similar condition being imposed on the subsequent purchaser.

ISBN: 978-1-83563-545-2

www.newgeneration-publishing.com

New Generation Publishing

Books are written in different ways and styles. This book is written colloquially. In other words, it's written as if we're having a conversation... albeit a one-way conversation. I've also tried to make it slightly interactive with the occasional bit of research on your behalf, which of course is totally optional!

I'd been thinking about writing this book for a while and I had often said to myself that writing a book can't be that hard... can it? I am now going to send out many grovelling apologies to all the writers out there who know more about writing books than I do. In other words, I was very wrong. As much, as I enjoyed writing this, I was very far off the mark.

This book is dedicated to Trevor Hurrell with lots of love and respect. In the face of adversity, Burrell (as we all knew him locally) just carried on. We were all blessed to have him in our lives.

PREFACE

I finally decided to begin to write this book the day after I took my mate Trevor to Addenbrooke's Hospital. His consultant wanted to see him about his ongoing condition and to discuss the results of a series of tests he had undergone. Unfortunately for him and for all of us, it turned out that he had bowel cancer. The consultant advised that he should have his whole bowel removed. I wanted to go and support him while he was meeting with his consultant. Trevor wanted me to stay in the hospital restaurant. I remember the look on his face when he had finished seeing his consultant. He didn't have to say anything... his face said it all. The image is still imprinted on my mind to this day.

INTRODUCTION

When I decided to travel with pretty much no plan as such, I had some interesting comments. Some were positive such as "Good for you", "You're so brave" and "Enjoy Yourself" *(It's Later Than You Think!)*. Look up the lyrics to the chorus of this Specials song. It's quite apt.

Then there were the negative ones like, "Why are you doing this?", "Aren't you scared?" and "What if something happens to you?" Yes, of course there was an element of fear and apprehension, but I really wanted to explore the world. I wanted to explore myself – to find out who I was. I just had to do it. I needed the room and space to grow. It was the case then, and is still the case now. It's a world full of wonderful choices, opportunities and adventures.

On the flip side, there was also the fear of doing nothing, of doing the same old boring things day in and day out. It's that thought of feeling old and shackled before my time and being trapped by circumstances. If I stayed in one place, I wouldn't find any answers. So, I had to get out there, so to speak. Of course, it's different for everyone.

Personally, staying in one place wasn't the life for me.

So, one Sunday morning, I was waiting in my car (in jolly Wood Green, next to the Haringey Civic Centre) for my mother to emerge from her usual Sunday morning church visit. I sat thinking about the 'fear' and 'bravery' aspect of life itself and what I was about to embark on. I asked myself these two questions. What is fear and what is bravery? My thoughts took a wander down memory lane to a book by Dale Carnegie called *How to Stop Worrying and Start Living*, which I read quite early on in my teens along with *How to Win Friends and Influence People*. In and amongst all this was the age-old saying, *'Feel the fear and do it anyway'*. I realised that for me, bravery and fear both spelled out the same thing...

> *Bravery is overcoming your fear. In my mind, in order to be brave, there is always an element of fear and worry which is a normal occurrence. One does not exist without the other.*

Looking back, I can relate travelling and exploring to the lyrics at the end of one of *Frank Turner's* songs – *I Am Disappeared*. It's such a great song... when you get a few minutes, have a listen! Or better still, look it up now on YouTube. At the end of the song there are a couple of lines that say that the roads are rivers of tarmac across the country and the world. He goes on to relate them to arteries in the body. When I relate it to myself, I see them as global arteries – global roads. He further goes on to say that the blood cells in the arteries are a reference to us; that we are all on a journey to somewhere, or in some cases, journeys to nowhere.

Whenever I am travelling, by car, bus, aeroplane and boat or even sitting in a cafe people-watching, I often wonder where these people are going and why they are going to their particular destinations. Is it work, pleasure, escaping a situation, etc? Who knows? Are they going to a chosen destination or is it a journey they don't really want to be a part of but a necessary journey nevertheless?

These days, when I fly anywhere and have been lucky to have a window seat or to evade a snoring passenger, I often look out of the window and imagine these scenarios with everyone playing out their own life plan, good and bad. I would even imagine animals on their own journey, dealing with their own trials and tribulations. It might seem a bizarre train of thought but it really gets me thinking about society and how the overwhelming majority of us follow a seemingly similar path.

There also seems to be a fear of not being accepted and branded weird unless we think the way that others do. In essence, we are all part of a tribe. We are communal creatures or, if you like, pack animals. I suppose it's the survival instinct in us. However, I've always seen myself as someone who is always looking into situations from the outside. I've never really had that wanting or need to belong to any cultural or social order. People who don't understand this view would label you as strange or odd or as a threat. In essence, for me it is their insecurities coming through in the form of wanting to control situations they come into contact with.

I suppose that in being part of the human race, we are produced over and over again (like a production line) and none of us are the same. It's both a physical and mental cycle. Life is made up from a series of jigsaw pieces. They are pieces of knowledge and experiences. As our own life moves forward, a picture emerges of who we are. Ultimately, most people want to belong or aspire to some kind of social or cultural group, which for me is not important. In my eyes, it's a social fear of not being accepted. With all that said, life should be an adventure to...

SEARCH FOR THE REAL "YOU" WITHIN YOURSELF

Some people know themselves early on in life, whereas there are others who are merely still waiting to evolve into the person they will become.

I hope you enjoy the read as much as I enjoyed the experience!

FIRST STEPS

We know a lot about the past; our own past, our family's past, our society's past, our cultural past and the past of virtually everything. In a way, it's there for us to learn from... not to make the same mistakes that others have made. However, the future is a different *kettle of fish* (that's an odd phrase don't you think – *kettle of fish?* I'll let you search the meaning of that and its origin on the internet). Can you see what I mean? Even that phrase has a past!

Whereas the past can be full of minute detail, the future is still to be experienced, still to be written as something that has not yet happened. It's a bit like John Locke's *Tabala Rasa 1689* – an empty sheet to be written on as experiences and learning develops. Again, I'll let you search up John Locke as well... it's an interesting theory and I kind of get where he's coming from.

Life is a funny thing really and more often than not, it has a way of sorting itself out. How this happens I have no idea. Mind you, there are those who believe that divine intervention is the answer. It might be... it might not be. Who knows? As for me, wherever the wind tends to blow, I'll go with it. If it feels right, I'll do it and if it doesn't feel right, then obviously I won't. It's as simple as that. I suppose I'm easy-going. Always have been and probably always will be! However, there are some limits and there's definitely a time to say "No!"

Some time ago I decided to throw caution to the wind. Just bear with me on this. By that I mean I started to look at situations and people around me. I went to various friends' and relatives' weddings, people who were ultimately getting mortgages, pension plans, having kids etc – you know how it is. I watched people at work, in the street and on the tube, all rushing around as if there was no tomorrow. It was almost as if the world was about to end. This was especially evident around Christmas, New Year's Eve, Mother's Day, Valentine's Day etc. There were people on the phone having arguments with friends or partners and airing their dirty washing in public. I have to say, listening to those conversations was very entertaining and in my defence, Your Honour, I didn't really have much of a choice. These people were so loud! I would sit around in cafés and pubs listening to suited up individuals talking on their newly acquired Motorola bricks, which were the state of the art in those days. They were grunting 'business'. I would often sit there and think, "What a load of male genitalia", if you get my drift! I must admit that whenever I hear or read the word 'business', I want to curl up into a ball and jump around just like John Cleese did in the *Fawlty Towers* episode called *The Psychiatrist*. If you haven't seen it, watch it! It definitely has to be on your list of 1001 things to watch before you die!

Anyway, I digress. I tend to do that, as you will no doubt see. I pretty much observed everything and I still do. It really isn't a conscious action. It just happens. I began to mull over this word 'Life', as we all do at some point of our lives. I came to the rapid conclusion that I didn't want to be on this emotional and materialistic roller coaster. I wanted to do things on my terms and not be restricted by an individual or any corporation or indeed, by any institution. I didn't want to just exist and drift into some kind of mediocrity. I wanted to live and enjoy life!

So, with all these thoughts floating around, I decided that I wanted to go 'off grid', so to speak. I came to the decision that I was going to embark on a journey somewhere... anywhere. It didn't really matter where. All I knew was that I had to get away from Palmers Green and the humdrum existence of what could possibly lie spread-eagled before me, stealthily enticing me, and pulling me towards it. I didn't want to conform to other people's expectations. I wanted to be released and have the freedom and choice that life had to offer and not be tied down mentally and physically. In a nutshell, that was really it! To live and exist without the restriction that others put on you, whether intentionally or unintentionally.

However, three little problems had to be sorted out. The initial problem was which country was going to have the pleasure of my company first. Well, that was relatively easy. I thought I would go to Israel as a good starting point. The second problem was, when was I going? That wasn't particularly hard either. I worked as a telephone engineer and in those days (1987) we were paid on a weekly basis, which meant that I only had to give a week's notice. I found myself a few travel agent, bucket shop phone numbers in *Timeout* magazine and rang them. I managed to find a one-way ticket to Tel Aviv for £69, which was cheap but not cheap enough! The airline was called Arkia (personally I'd never heard of them at the time) and was flying from Gatwick. So, after work, I caught the tube down to Great Portland Street and ended up going down into a basement to pay and collect this ticket to take me away from a life of impending predictability.

In this one shabby, smoke-filled room, was a man dressed in a blue stained suit. He was looking at a flickering green computer screen and having a civil chat to someone on the phone. He motioned me in with his cigarette of all things, and pointed to a chair which looked like it had been given to a teething baby crocodile to chew on. I sat there looking around thinking, "Am I really going to buy a ticket from this bloke?" He looked like he would sell his own mother for a profit. Ah yes, my mum! How was I going to tell her? That was my third little problem. Well actually, it was potentially a massive problem. How was she going to take it? I hadn't given it much thought till now. She would not be very happy. That was a dead cert! I eventually bought the ticket, which I hoped was legitimate, handed over my hard-earned cash and got out of that chimney of a room as quickly as I could. I was now armed with my ticket to fly out in two weeks. In fact, the date I had picked was Wednesday 16th September... the day before my birthday.

So, I had booked my ticket to Tel Aviv, on what I hoped was not a Mickey Mouse airline. I had my escape departure date from this 9 to 5 existence. In the meantime, I joined the International Youth Hostel Association (IYH) and I still hadn't told my mum! Now this was something I was not looking forward to. I just had these images of it going pear-shaped, my mum breaking down and crying and saying, "Don't go." Definitely not something I wanted to experience.

At this time, we lived in quite a big house in Palmers Green, more commonly known on the strip as 'Palmers Greek', for obvious reasons. My dad had died when I was fourteen, so for years it was just my mum, my older brother and me. My brother had got hitched and moved out, whereupon I'd moved into his much larger room. It was Christmas come early. I felt very protective of my mum like any self-respecting child would be, but I had to get out and experience life for myself and not stay in a safe bubble, where everything was on tap. Anyway, I had kind of discussed it with her at various times before I'd booked my ticket. I was just testing the waters but hadn't really made any decisions about it. When I did eventually tell her, to my amazement and in between huge waves of guilt gushing over me, she was brilliant! I tried to fight back the tears but it was no use... the floodgates opened for both of us. It was a very emotional moment. She had said to me that she had sensed I was restless and that I would be off somewhere, just like my brother had done years before. She was really excited for me, especially when I told her that I was flying out to Israel. My brother expressed his usual excitement in the phrase "You lucky, lucky bastard! Can I come?" He'd given me his old, red, aluminium framed rucksack along with his sleeping bag and he bought me a Swiss Army knife. He said it would come in useful. He was not wrong, it was very useful – the best thing ever!

Once everything was pretty much sorted out, I thought it best to get cholera and typhoid jabs, given that I wasn't exactly sure where I would be ending up. I made an appointment with my GP and he gave me the jabs on the same visit. Apparently, this was OK to do. Who was I to argue? Now, needles and I are on different sides of all fences that presently exist. In other words, I don't like needles! I walked into my doctor's surgery as nervous as hell, prepared with a hip flask, three layers of Y-fronts and an incontinence pad, just to accommodate any fallout.

I looked my GP in the eye and asked him to be gentle with me. He cheekily laughed and replied with the imposing needle in his hand, "I bet you say that to all the boys!" A dodgy reply if you ask me, especially when there was a pool of hot steaming sweat collecting nicely at my feet. He deposited the goods into my arm, which seemed to take forever and I even had to pay him £10 for the privilege. That evening, I started to feel ill and I was expecting something to happen. I had been warned by my GP that it was a live vaccine and that there could be side effects. My arm ached and I had a fever the entire night. I felt a bit tender around the edges but in a manner of speaking, I had weathered the storm by the morning.

Talking of vaccines, a good friend of mine called Lisa, who flew out to meet me in Israel, had an interesting encounter with the Tamiflu vaccine. We'll catch up with her later on. It was around the time when some agencies were predicting a bird flu pandemic and it was all over the news at the time. People were starting to panic (as was Lisa) so she decided to try and get hold of the Tamiflu vaccine. As it happened, she found a supplier who was based in Turkey of all places and she bought £300 worth at 1am. When she told me I thought the whole thing was a little bit suspect. I obviously wasn't the only one thinking along those lines either. As a result, she was contacted by the fraud squad and they questioned her about the purchase. You can imagine the conversation!

The day had come for me to leave. It was a Wednesday, and my flight was leaving from Gatwick Airport at 10.20pm. My brother picked me up after an emotional farewell with my mum. As we left, he made sure I had everything. We arrived at the steps of Turnpike Lane tube station, where he promptly pushed me out of his old, beaten-up, Japanese relic of a car. We had the usual chat about looking after myself and to ring Mum when I could. I told him to keep an eye on Mum. Then it was a quick hug and that was it. I was gone.

"So, here it begins", I told myself, "You're on your own now, sonny". I then somewhat nervously bought my train ticket to Victoria Station. I wandered, fully laden with all my possessions (which believe me, wasn't much) down the ancient wooden escalators onto the deserted platform. I eventually got to Gatwick Airport via Victoria Station in good time and started looking around for the Arkia check-in desk. Then I saw it conveniently stuck in a remote corner. "So it does exist", I thought. Sometimes when you get an idea into your head, it's difficult to dislodge. Maybe it was a sign of things to come.

It was very near the El Al check-in desk and I was inching nearer and nearer in a snakelike fashion towards the check-in desk. This was when I became aware of a rather strong, pungent smell. It was so strong I had to take a step back as if someone had stuck a tube of superglue under my nose causing the room to spin. That was a slight exaggeration, but it was bloody strong! I then realised this smell was wafting over from a middle-aged man to my left, who had something resembling a black Stetson hat, a long, thick, black coat and black trousers. Over his eyes, he was sporting a pair of thick, black rimmed glasses which complemented his long, grey, thicket-like beard. Initially, I couldn't quite work out what was hanging from his midriff. It turns out that they were tassels hanging down under his white shirt, which was under his black jumper. I looked closer and noticed large beads of sweat escaping from his forehead. Could it be that this sweet aroma was even too much for his trickling sweat? It probably couldn't wait to get away from its host! I knew how it felt! I just hoped that I wasn't sitting next to him. Can you imagine having to deal with the smell for 5 hours and no relief except for the aircraft's escape hatch or even the toilet? Thinking about it, perhaps a toilet getaway was not such a good idea given what toilets can be like.

I eventually checked in, got myself a quick drink and decided to go through to departures and passport control. Now, I was warned about Israeli security so I thought I would get it over with. They don't mess about. As it happens it wasn't too bad. I thought it was pretty much straightforward. I had all the usual questions such as where are you going, where are you staying, do you know anyone in Israel? Are you carrying anything for anyone? Are you carrying a rocket launcher? A Kalashnikov? Any pipe bombs? Semtex? High quality weed killer? And the questions went on. It gets to a point where you just want to say "Yes, I've got all that!" just to see what would happen. However, they were surprisingly OK with me taking my Swiss Army knife on board. I never did understand that. The searches and frisking were a lot easier. Standing upright with arms spread out and having someone rub their hands over me was no hardship. I had decided at that point not to make any ambiguous comments. I thought it would be a wise move given the circumstances. Mind you, I did check my pockets just to make sure nothing was taken out. Even worse, make sure nothing was put in! After all that excitement I was free to skip away and I did just that. I skipped through to the departure security, much to the disgust and dismay of the security personnel.

Oh well, it could have been worse – there was an hour's delay. I was in no hurry. So, I decided to do a bit of window shopping and people-watching. I remember watching this couple who were dressed to kill. By that, I mean they were dressed immaculately. Over the top in my view, but hey, who am I to say anything? If they feel that they want to be noticed by dressing up in all the latest fashions and it makes them feel better, then good luck to them. However, I never could understand it and still don't understand it. I suppose some people are happy in the skin they're in, and others have to mask it.

I started looking at the prices of aftershave, perfume and clothes – pretty much everything. All of it was branded and all of it was way over the top in terms of price. I suppose people want to be seen in these ludicrously expensive garments and wafting scents. It doesn't appeal to me but hey, each to their own. I always remember kids at school turning up with ridiculously expensive Adidas bags, whereupon some would say either "Welcome to the club", or "What a tosser". I would always lean towards the latter.

After another half an hour of aimlessly walking around the departure lounge with a cup of coffee which interestingly cost more than my plane ticket, I decided to do a quality control check on the male toilets. Yep, you read it right - a quality control toilet exercise just to pass the time. Some people like to read books and shop like some of the aforementioned individuals, and others like to take part in constructive activities. I'd used one of the toilets earlier and it was rank. There was bright yellow piss everywhere, which was complemented by a white tiled background. It was as if someone swallowed a dozen radioactive travel sickness pills and completely missed the urinal or alternatively, he was just leaving his calling card. Either way it smelt like mucking out time in our local equestrian centre. Luckily for me, I heard my flight being called to board, so there was going to be no quality control taking place today.

I eventually made my way onto the plane and settled down into my window seat. It was around 11.30pm and everyone looked worn out so I was hoping it would be a quiet flight. I spotted my sweaty friend with the Stetson hat seated near the toilets at the back... the further away the better! There would be no way I could to hold my breath for the entire five-hour flight.

The flight was pretty much uneventful. It went very smoothly and not a whiff from a certain individual. In saying that, I did notice the on-board flight attendants flapping and rushing towards the other end of the plane with several oxygen cylinders and a cart full of smelling salts, pulled by a Shire horse answering to the name of Colin. I can't be sure but I reckon I must have been dreaming!

However, as the flight was nearing Tel Aviv Airport, I peered out of the window at the miniscule lights below. I had this sudden feeling of pain; as if someone had smacked me around the head with a hot, fully loaded, bag of greasy chips. I had this sudden realisation of WHAT THE FUCK WAS I DOING? I'd resigned from a perfectly good job, had around £700 of traveller's cheques and $100 in cash, which quite honestly wouldn't last very long if I wasn't careful. I had nowhere to stay, I didn't know anyone and the list went on. I think most of us have had that feeling of doubt at some point in our lives and this was my extremely brief flutter with self-doubt. What made it more interesting was the fact that I was in mid-air with nowhere else to go; but this was what I wanted. I wanted to experience the unknown, both physically and mentally. It was an opportunity to explore without answering to anyone and getting away from everything that I found restricting. And that was it! There was no more doubt. It probably lasted no more than about ten seconds but time enough to reaffirm that what I was doing was the right thing for me. It's not everyone's cup of tea.

Some like to play it safe by staying where they are, surrounding themselves with people and material things and being in a system. What I was doing was also a system but it was my own system, my own chaos, my own choices and above all... it was my own life. To get an idea of where I am coming from with this, listen to another song by Frank Turner called *Photosynthesis*. The lyrics are brilliant. In my view and in hindsight, it pretty much sums up how I was feeling at the time and to be honest, I still feel it. Anyway, I broke out (sounds like a prison but that's how it felt) and it was the best feeling ever.

TEL AVIV AND JAFFA

We landed at Ben Gurion Airport at around 6.30am local time to the rapturous applause of all the passengers including Colin the Shire horse, who was neighing with delight. It never ceases to amaze me when that happens. It's a lovely thing and you kind of get swept along with the euphoria of it all and before long you're clapping, screaming and throwing your Y-fronts towards the Captain's cabin, while riotously singing a song by Tom Robinson called *Cabin Boy*.

Once the excitement died down, I remembered that I had to navigate the infamous Israeli security, which I was strangely looking forward to but I must admit, I was a tiny bit let down. I had all the usual questions thrown at me. They were pretty much the same ones I had earlier but these were being asked with the backdrop of soldiers lovingly fondling their Uzi machine guns. They did get a bit suspicious, especially when they noticed my ex-army and navy munitions bag in which I kept my camera, Sony Walkman, Swiss Army knife etc. They had a rummage... well actually they just emptied it onto the table and pushed things around like a disinterested child with their food saying, "What is this shit you've given me to eat?" My rucksack was also abused pretty much in the same manner. When they had finished, I heard the words, "Welcome to Israel". I was then left to repack everything. I obviously ticked one or two terrorist boxes. So that was that. I was little bit miffed that I was not taken into a small grey coloured room with a 2-way mirror, a 1000-watt interrogation lamp and a wooden table where someone had carved out 'Help' with the aid of a 6-foot machete. Not even a whiff of a frisk. How disappointing!

Having successfully repacked my rucksack somewhat hurriedly, I left the airport and waited at the bus stop. I sat musing through the International Youth Hostel (IYH) book looking for somewhere to stay. There was a choice of one. As I read the words, 'book in advance is recommended' (which I hadn't done) two young guys with well-used rucksacks planted themselves next to me. They had heavy Northern Irish accents and if I closed my eyes, I could pretend I was talking to Jake Burns from *Stiff Little Fingers*. We started talking, mainly about Israeli security, like you would, and then about accommodation. It turns out they were also looking for the IYH so we hatched a plan to get a room together (not in that way I might add) as it would be cheaper. This is what we hoped.

The bus arrived and the first thing I noticed was the cleanliness of it. This was luxury compared to the buses back home, where we had to take our own needle and cotton to sew up the bus seats before we sat down. We politely asked the bus driver if he went anywhere near the IYH. The answer was a grunt and a nod which I soon realised as time went on, was the common verbal currency in these parts, as well as in others.

We eventually came to a stop and the driver shouted "OSTEL" in a similar tone of voice to an overhead, low-flying Vulcan bomber at an air show. Luckily, we were the only ones on this sanitised bus, otherwise there could have been a huge potential for a spot of chaos, given the ferocity in the driver's voice. We stumbled out of the bus and stood outside a building with the IYH triangle clinging to the wall for dear life. We naturally assumed that this must be it. In we went and booked ourselves a room for one night, just to get our bearings. The guys were looking to stay on a kibbutz, which is what a lot of travellers did, but I wasn't really looking into that option yet, if at all. They were going to seek out a kibbutz office to make arrangements to book themselves into a kibbutz. I, on the other hand, decided to find myself a cheaper place to stay as I thought that the IYH was a tad expensive. To be fair, the room wasn't too bad. It was a good size, had two sets of bunk beds, a sink and a naturally air-conditioned chest of drawers and matching wardrobe. These were things I was not going to use. I was planning to live out of my rucksack with all of its personal attributes which included stale aromas, if you get my meaning! That's why I had my own stash of washing powder. The toilet and showers were a shared experience but they were clean, which surprised me. They must have been regularly cleaned.

It was around 9am by the time we booked in and had a quick wash, so we decided to have some breakfast. We found our way into the dining area accompanied by the dulcet tones of Leonard Cohen's *Suzanne*. It was drifting lazily through the internal music system, which I thought was a nice touch. For me, that was a very 'hostel type' welcome. All it needed to top it off would have been a cannabis vending machine with complimentary razor blades. Jokes aside, I do like a bit of Leonard Cohen.

Now... back to the breakfast. Listening to my best ever Northern Irish buddies trying to get a coffee and some toast was most amusing. Their accent was very heavy and even I had to double-check what they were saying at times. In saying that, they found my North London accent equally incomprehensible. It must have been hell for the guy behind the counter. He kept saying, "Excuse me" and "Can you repeat that, sir" in a kind of dodgy American but not American accent. I have to say, it was very funny! I suggested that they should have a notebook so that they could draw what they wanted or grunt or point. After our brief and rather expensive breakfast, I went off armed with a free tourist map of Tel Aviv which I had picked up from the airport. I wanted to explore Tel Aviv a little and to find a cheaper hostel to stay in. As I had said earlier, the IYH was quite pricey. The guys went off to find the Kibbutz Office.

I started walking around taking everything in, including the heavy military presence and made my way to the Tel Aviv coast. Israel was and still is largely on high security alert due to its relationships with the Arab states surrounding it. Both men and women are conscripted into the army to complete National Service. Only the male and female Orthodox Jews are exempt from National Service, otherwise everyone was expected to do it, which would normally last for around two years. Having conscripted women on the streets was something I'd never seen before. I have to admit that having the female warrior recruits on the streets was a rather picturesque sight. It reminded me of Iron Maiden's *Women in Uniform*. It was a good job I was wearing my bib!

It was starting to get hot and it wasn't quite 10.30 yet. It was great to be away doing my own thing and not having to surrender to the powers that be at work. I'm talking about my former employers. That feeling seemed a lifetime away, although it was only a couple of days ago. It felt strange, but I was apprehensively excited and was definitely enjoying it. I noticed that the signs were a mixture of Hebrew, Arabic and English, which was very handy. As I walked, I came across a number of hostels which all looked equally dodgy, but I popped in regardless, asking about availability and cost. They were all cheaper than the IYH with some beds being available and if there weren't any beds, they suggested that I could share with someone. This was certainly an interesting concept and definitely a bit of a lottery. How would that work? Would I be entertaining a local family of insects? Would it be a male or female bed-mate? Would I end up spooning someone or being spooned? Would it be a head-to-toe event? Would I be examining someone's corns or cracked dry skin on the soles of their feet? Or worse still, a pungent assortment of cheesy aromas rising into the humid Israeli evening and when it was finally fermented, would it be ready for a tasting session in the morning? So many questions, all of which I felt that someone else would be better qualified to experience and report back with a simple account.

Thinking about it, you could even include a scratch and sniff section just to make it a real remote encounter! Imagine that! What an absolutely genius idea!

I eventually got to the coast and I was greeted with the most reaffirming view and smell of the sea. This had just confirmed that leaving the UK behind and stepping into the unknown was the right thing to do. I started walking along the coastal road not knowing where the hell I was going. I consulted the map and started heading towards the Ramada Renaissance Hotel, which I could see in the hazy distance. The hotel is now called the Renaissance Hotel and has been bought by the Marriott.

On the way, I spotted a public telephone and decided to ring my mum to let her know that I had arrived safely. I reversed the charges like one does and reassured my mum that everything was fine and that the weather was great. She was happy with that. It also reminded me that I should ring Lisa to see if she was definitely coming over to the land of milk and honey.

When I eventually got to the Ramada Renaissance, I noticed a hostel opposite called the Gordon Hostel, which funnily enough was on the corner of Gordon Street. The two establishments couldn't be more contrasting. The Ramada Renaissance was clean and well-maintained with great toilets. How did I know, I hear you ask? Well as it happens, I used the hotel toilets just before I strolled into the Gordon Hostel. They were the most fantastic place to blow your minor and major auxiliary tanks and freshen up. I particularly liked the idea that they supplied fancy liquid soap and hand moisturising cream. I just walked in as if I owned the place, used the facilities and then casually walked out again. It was that easy. However, unfortunately for me, I wasn't staying there.

Mind you, a day or so later, I got talking to one of the doormen at the Ramada. He thought I was staying there but I said, pointing across the road, that I was a reluctant paying guest at the Gordon Hostel. He grimaced as I said that, which was quite funny and replied by saying that he had heard that it was a disgusting place. I agreed with him and said that it was my choice and that I was trying to save money. I mentioned how nice the toilets in the Ramada were compared to the Gordon. To my amazement, he said that he wouldn't challenge me if he saw me go into the toilets. He was as good as his word. He actually said that it was nice that I took the time to chat with him as most people who stayed at the Ramada didn't even acknowledge him, until they wanted something. My view is that we are all the same. No one is better than anyone else regardless of the jobs we all do or how much money we have. If I can give a compliment or bring a smile to at least one person every day, then I've done my bit for them. In other words, be respectful.

As I was saying, I looked at the Gordon Hostel from across the road and sauntered into the crumbling building, which needed a lot of tender loving care, and asked the usual questions. It turns out they had an opening for a bed sloth so I had a look. I was taken onto the first floor and through a couple of corridors with beds and sofas situated in various corners. Then I was told that this particular flea-ridden sofa, which you really wouldn't give to your own worst enemy, was being vacated tomorrow morning. As he was pointing to it, I couldn't believe that I was actually contemplating saying "Yes". I was even contemplating haggling on the price. I tried to knock him down but he wouldn't budge on the price. In saying that, it was cheap and ever so nasty, but I took it. In for a penny, in for a shekel! He looked really smug when I finally gave in and accepted. I asked myself, "How bad could it be?" as we shook hands on it. Well I suppose I was going to find out soon enough!

With *Mission Accomplished*... incidentally, a brilliant live album by The Rezillos recorded in Glasgow, I wandered down Gordon Street which was littered with shops which sold everything you could think of. I eventually stumbled into Dizengoff Square on Dizengoff Street. In the middle of this square was an odd-looking structure. Historically, the square was built in 1934 and was at street level. When I was there, it was elevated above Dizengoff Street to ease the traffic. Nowadays, Dizengoff Square is once again at street level. It is famous or infamous depending on how you look at it, for its fountain – *Fire and Water*. I was sitting on a bench looking at this collection of coloured cylinders and circles, when my curiosity got the better of me. I didn't have a travel guide book so I just had to ask someone what the hell it was.

As luck would have it, there were two women sitting on the same bench having a natter in Hebrew. I asked them what this structure was and fortunately for me they both spoke good English. I embarrassingly explained to them that I had only arrived in Israel that morning and my whole Hebrew vocabulary was limited to "Shalom". Hey, I was learning! We hit it off straight away and the conversation was very animated. They were only too willing to explain what the structure was and told me the best time to see it was at night, as there was often a sound and light show. Then these wonderful ladies casually informed me about places to see and cheap places to eat, which was handy.

The ladies fired loads of questions at me. Some of them were personal and some were quite general. To be honest, it was quite hard to get a word in, but we had a good, healthy chat. They asked me about what I had achieved so far, my plans for the future, was I Jewish and was I engaged or married? I told them that I had resigned from a perfectly good job to do my own thing. They both simultaneously nodded that knowing nod! They were probably thinking, "Bloody idiot! He could be making money but instead, he's dossing!" Alternatively, they could be thinking, "Ah bless, he's such a lovely lad!" Who knows what thoughts they were harbouring?

In saying that, they were very upfront with me, which was really quite refreshing. Apparently, they both had daughters that needed a husband and was I interested? I might add that this was all tongue in cheek. I answered the ladies by saying that there was only one snag. With a big grin on my face, I said to the ladies that I had been fighting off two other suitors with feathers, whilst being blindfolded and wearing nothing but a smile and a thong made of sandpaper. Otherwise, I would have possibly considered their kind offer. Obviously, I didn't put it quite that way.

By this point I was getting tired. I hadn't really had much sleep. In fact, I'd had no sleep at all. The heat wasn't doing me any favours either, so I attempted to crawl back to the IYH which, to my surprise, I found quite easily. I was so tired, that I collapsed onto the bottom bunk after contemplating the hike up to the top bunk and just fell asleep. I was woken in a middle of a dream in which it was raining feathers and thongs (it's funny how conversations with complete strangers translate into dreams). My rude awakening was courtesy of my Northern Irish fellow travellers. They had found themselves a kibbutz in the northern part of Israel, not far from Nazareth, and were leaving tomorrow. To celebrate, food and drinks were in order. We ended up having a falafel, salad and tahini in pitta bread from a stall. It was absolutely delicious... totally orgasmic. I hadn't had authentic falafels before. My brother had made them quite often at home and they were good, but these particular ones were something else. The only place in the UK that came near to the perfect falafel was in a restaurant called, The Falafel House in Belsize Park in London. To be honest, I'm not sure it's still there these days. Anyway, we ended up having a few beers and retired, somewhat merrily, to our respective bunks.

After a rather noisy and guttural night, we had breakfast. Once our rucksacks were packed and secured, we said our goodbyes and went our separate ways. I hadn't realised how heavy and sweaty a rucksack could get while walking a fair distance. Mine was relatively light and compact in comparison to others. I made it to the Gordon Hostel, checked in, dumped my rucksack next to my flea-ridden sofa which I could call mine for the next few days, and wandered out towards the beach. The hostel was literally opposite the beach. It was a great location and it was cheap, so I couldn't ask for more.

I could make out Jaffa in the distance and started walking. Jaffa is located at the southern end of Tel Aviv. It's an ancient port and is in the biblical stories of Solomon, Jonah and Saint Peter. Jaffa apparently also boasts mythological stories of Andromeda and Perseus, which is something I find interesting. However, when I first saw the town of Jaffa on the map, my mind went straight to oranges, as it would. I remember having them as a kid. Evidently, Jaffa was the original home of Jaffa oranges, which were seedless. Hence, the word on the streets was that all men who were infertile were called *Jaffas*.

Historically, the old town of Jaffa has various names. It's known as Yafo in Hebrew, Yafa in Arabic and Japho or Joppa as a biblical reference. I walked along the coastal road and noticed the gloriously sandy beach with its Baywatch-type inhabitants sporting their swimwear, screaming with joy or just lying down soaking up the sun's rays. I can never to this day understand why people lay on the beach day after day, inviting all the sun's harmful rays and ending up with damaged skin or at worst, skin cancer. The sea looked so refreshing that I jumped down onto the beach, took off my boating plimsolls (another ex-Army and Navy purchase) and walked barefoot like Sandie Shaw through the gentle lapping waves. It was bliss! At that moment my friend Claire popped into my head. Years ago, she had mentioned in a conversation that she had walked along the beach in Cyprus (incidentally, a twelve-hour ferry crossing across the Mediterranean Sea) while listening to Siouxsie and the Banshees.

Having found walking on the beach hard work, I climbed back up onto the pavement and eventually made it to Jaffa. I unintentionally stumbled into Abrasha Park where the Statue of Faith sits. It's the highest point in Jaffa and the views were just breathtaking. Taking everything into consideration such as the heat, the sea, the blue sky, the salty sea air and loads of fig trees, I could honestly say that I was in heaven! In my opinion, this was an idyllic spot, so I decided to sit on a shaded bench and devour a grapefruit which I had bought earlier. With the aid of my Swiss Army knife, I began to artistically carve it open. My hands were very sticky after eating the grapefruit, so I washed them with bottled water and began to read a book that I had 'borrowed' from the hostel. There was a shelf full of books and the idea was that it was an exchange but I had no books to exchange so I took one and I told the shelf that I would return it once I had finished with it. The shelf didn't respond... I wasn't in the least bit surprised! I spent most of the rest of the day reading Jeffery Archer's *A Quiver Full of Arrows*. Beggars can't be choosers but it was ok.

At this point I was getting a tad peckish, so I started to meander towards Jaffa Port, not really knowing where the hell I was going. I was just following my nose – that's the beauty of it. Just in case you're wondering, I'm not referring to my nose, although I must say I do have a beautiful nose. I'm referring to what I was doing... pottering about. I found a small supermarket and bought myself two microscopic croissants and some more fruit. There was nothing cheaper. I had to watch the money side of things. I didn't want to run out of money and end up selling my body too soon.

I left the supermarket feeling pretty chuffed with my so-called bargains and began walking into Old Jaffa. As I was just looking around and generally minding my own business, I was being eyed up by the locals. They were probably thinking tourist equals money. That unnerved me a bit, but I soon got used to that as time went on. I even had the local dogs giving me the eye, wondering what part of my body they could start chewing on first. Needless to say, I made my way back onto the main coastal road via the port and headed back to the hostel with all my limbs intact and in good working order.

As I approached the hostel, I was once again in awe of its brilliant location and view. It could not have been better. I walked into the crumbling hostel, dodging any falling parts that decided to test my reflexes. I put the remainder of the fruit I had bought into the fridge thinking that I could have it for breakfast tomorrow and then collapsed onto my five-star sofa. Did I see dust rising? Or was it a community of homeless fleas soon to be claiming housing benefit as I flopped onto the sofa? Probably both! Lying there tracing the cracks on the ceiling, I thought I had better ring Lisa to see if she was coming. I would have to get a couple of public telephone coin tokens, which had a hole in the middle and a parallel slot either side of the hole. I was able to get them from the hostel's reception to make the call. I didn't think reversing the charges would go down too well with Lisa's parents. I managed to make the call after spending a few minutes fathoming out the whole process. I spoke to Lisa, who said she was booked on a flight to Tel Aviv. She had a two-week ticket and was due out in a couple of days. I was pleased she was coming. So, I had a couple of days to get to know Tel Aviv better, which was good.

I was hungry. In fact, I was starving, so I thought I'd take a walk down to Dizengoff Square to get a bite to eat. As I dodged all these well-dressed locals heading out for the evening, I finally made it to the square, where my eyes became bigger than my stomach. You could smell and even feel the falafels and shawarmas creeping up both nostrils. Even the colour of the salad on display was impressive and at around a shekel and a half for a falafel, I couldn't go wrong. The good thing about these stalls was that you were given your falafels in round pitta bread and the rest was self-service. Well, say no more. This was going to be a military exercise in loading up the previously mentioned pitta bread. The guy behind the stall kept looking at me, probably wondering what on earth I was doing. I strategically placed my tomatoes and cucumbers in my pitta bread and then piled on whatever else I could get my hands on. I think I might have put Mount Kilimanjaro to shame with my organic construction. Anyway, I demolished my meal while I was seated on a low external wall while facing the fountain. As I mentioned earlier, the fountain was the main focus of the square and there were lots people pretty much doing the same thing. I could honestly say I was totally stuffed and as a result, I was quite thirsty, so I waddled over to the supermarket and bought a small carton of chocolate milk. Over the next few days this would be my evening meal routine. I was also able to monitor how much money I would be spending each day.

I sat there drinking my choccy milk and people-watching (something I still enjoy doing). Without any warning, The Beatles' *Paperback Writer* came blaring over the square's resident PA system. The atmosphere in the square changed. People were excited and started pointing at the fountain. Being new to these parts, I had no idea what was going on. I actually asked an elderly couple what was happening and they replied by pointing at the fountain. In fact, everyone was pointing at the fountain. No words, just pointing. I wasn't telepathic! The whole thing reminded me of a William Shatner *Star Trek* episode, when some kind of planetary god wearing a very questionable outfit and dodgy make up would emerge from the centre of the earth. It was totally surreal.

Within seconds, the multi-coloured fountain started revolving and jets of water shot out from the middle, while a series of different coloured lights flashed on and off. As all this was going on, multiple jets of water shot vertically into the air, changing height and shape from the edges. All the lights and jets of water moved in time with the music. I was watching this for a good thirty minutes and I have to admit, I was mesmerised. It was almost as bad as watching a washing machine in our local laundrette. I was wondering when the fire part of this fountain would grace us with its presence. Alas, there was no fire. I felt hard done by and cheated out of an experience of a lifetime! I started beating my chest and wailing like one does in disappointment. Why call it the Water and Fire fountain when there was clearly no sign of any pyrotechnic activity? Is there no justice in the world? I suppose listening to the Beatles was some kind of consolation. The crowd were even singing along to some of the songs. The biggest response from this singing mass of individuals was when *All You Need is Love* was played. If the truth be known, I actually enjoyed the experience in a rather strange and masochistic way but I will never admit it publicly. I have my reputation to uphold...NOT!

I eventually strolled back to the hostel expecting to get some sleep but how wrong could I have been? Very wrong indeed! I soon found out that the owners of the hostel were holding a residents/dossers gathering on the rooftop garden and all residents and dossers were invited. Who was I to refuse? The beer was cheap and there were empty packets of Lays crisps lying around in various crevices of the roof. I'd obviously missed out on those freebies but I have to say that the view from the top of the hostel, coupled with the cool sea breeze, was just incredible. I managed to get talking to a couple of Dutch girls whose English was much better than my Dutch. Come to think of it, their command of the English language was better than mine!

They had been in Israel for about a week and they had booked themselves into a kibbutz and were leaving in the morning. They were quite funny really, cracking jokes all the time, which was great. They told me what to watch out for, where to shop, what to see and most importantly, to count my change. We chatted for a bit but by this time I was starting to tire. I just wanted to get some sleep, so I wished them luck and I retired as gracefully as I could onto my luxury sofa, hoping that it was not going to be a long night. In fact, it was an OK type of night. There was a bit of scratching here and there which was offset and accompanied by certain lumps in the sofa. The lumps were the size of golf balls which every now and then explored the lower end of my nether regions when I was trying to get comfy. This was also supplemented with a German Stuka type of mosquito, making high-pitched dive-bombing sounds around me and having a few successful hits.

Having woken rather early and after having a quick read (something I often did) I made my way to the shared bathroom and began washing my face. I looked at the mirror and I saw three small mounds on my forehead, which were more or less in a straight line. They weren't mosquito bites but a series of flea bites. Freddy Flea was obviously carrying a metre-long spirit level, marking its territory on my forehead. I wonder if Vyvyan in *The Young Ones* used this method. So now that I was Vyvyan's potential stunt double, I made my way to the fridge to reclaim my fruit.

It's now audience/reader participation time... You need to make a prediction. What happened next? Well, let me phrase it in a simple but diplomatic way. Some bastard had nicked my fruit! I don't know what I'd expected really. Some light-fingered opportunist was always going to help themselves, weren't they? That was definitely a lesson learnt.

Over the next couple of days, I just pottered about Tel Aviv, which I really enjoyed. I spent time on the beach reading, observing people and generally just chilling out in whatever shade I could find. I was determined not to get sunburnt. I wanted to avoid the red face syndrome. I did not want to resemble a *Ko-Chi-No-Golo*. It's a Greek word and if you haven't worked it out yet, I've written it out phonetically. It's a common nickname for those red-faced and well-grilled tourists. The word translates into 'red arse' and is associated with a baboon's red bum. I'll let your imagination engage and run riot with that image.

At times, I even listened to music on my very trendy blue and purple Sony Walkman. In fact, it was so trendy that it was featured in a film called *Blinded By The Light*. Just in case you're wondering, I'm referring to the model and colour, not my particular Sony Walkman. Incidentally, I still have it and it still works! Anyway, it's an absolutely brilliant film. It's a true story based on the influence of Bruce Springsteen's music and lyrics experienced by an older teenage Asian boy at college. It's certainly worth watching!

Going back to the Sony Walkman, I thought that it was one of the best inventions EVER! Now it's the Apple iPod, various MP3 devices and phones that have this honour. They take up so little space whereas the Walkman was a little bit bulky and you had to carry the cassette tapes, which took up even more space.

Anyway, it was relaxing and I was doing my own thing, which is what I wanted. I kept changing location and at one point I ended up on a bench on the promenade behind the Ramada Hotel. It was really quite busy with lots of people milling around.

I was just sitting there minding my own business and reading my book, when I looked up and noticed two rough-looking men glancing in my direction. At the time I thought nothing of it and carried on reading until I looked up again and saw one of the men walk past me. As he walked by, he was looking directly at me. I carried on reading but by this time I was becoming a tiny bit suspicious, especially when the other guy strolled towards me. He looked at me and then momentarily looked past me and nodded. Suddenly, it dawned on me that the other guy was behind me and that the nod was some kind of signal. I didn't wait to find out how this was going to unfold, so I jumped up, looked behind me and saw the other guy just a few feet from where I was sitting. I ran into a crowd of people, knowing that running was the right thing to do and that I was not imagining it. I was going to be a victim of a mugging. I casually looked behind me and caught glimpses of these two guys. It seemed that they were having an argument in public, gesturing with their arms and in full view of everyone. They were definitely not happy bunnies. I'm assuming that they had singled me out as I was on my own, I wasn't tanned and I stood out like a fully clad Manchester United fan in the middle of The Kop with a munitions bag. I didn't blend in but as time went on, I knew that I would. On hindsight that was a lucky escape. My senses had certainly been heightened since I'd started travelling, that's for sure. A good thing in my opinion!

This reminds me of a very similar situation but nowhere near as dangerous that involved my brilliant friend Trevor, who as I mentioned earlier, is sadly no longer with us. I have so many great memories of him. He is sorely missed by everyone that knew him. To his friends he was known as Burrell. One year we booked a very late break to the only place we could find for the dates we had – Benidorm. To cut a long story short (a brilliant song by Spandau Ballet) we stood out like sore thumbs. Initially, we were both given all sorts of free tickets to clubs etc. You get the picture? Maybe you've experienced this sort of thing yourselves. Anyway, as time went on, we didn't have any more leaflets shoved into our faces. This was most likely due to the fact that we had tans but also possibly due to what we were wearing. Burrell looked like a Spanish waiter going off to work, dressed in a white shirt and black drainpipe jeans. I was dressed in black dungarees and looked like a Spanish version of Kevin Rowland (*Dexys Midnight Runners*) who had just finished slogging his guts out on the fields. We both resembled the locals. All in all, that wasn't a bad thing really.

After my little near mugging experience, I decided to head into the centre of Tel Aviv and just potter. The probability of getting lost was actually quite remote. The coastal road and the sea became my beacon for getting back to the hostel as well as some other landmarks, which became a good habit. This is something I eventually did automatically. I came across a busy and bustling city which I hadn't really noticed before. Well, I probably did notice but it hadn't really registered. It was teeming with restaurants, cafés, shops of all kinds and food stalls. The aromas that were wafting into the warm September afternoon air from the stalls were making me drool, just like one of Pavlov's dogs. Having nowhere in particular to go, I wandered into an indoor food market and noticed the abundant colours on offer to the eye. Just trying to take all this in was truly intoxicating. I couldn't get enough of it; the colours mixed in with the smell of the spices and the fruit was just fantastic. Visually, it was like a kaleidoscope with all the colours blending into each other. Isn't it amazing that something so simple can have an everlasting imprint on your memory?

Having survived another blissful night on my own personal sofa, the next day was spent pottering on the beach, reading and generally doing nothing... again! Most enjoyable! Lisa was flying out from the UK that night and was expected around 11pm. That morning, I'd managed to secure a similar type of flea-bitten sofa for Lisa as there was nothing else available. I wasn't sure how Lisa would react. I didn't have much of a choice, but I suppose it would have to do.

Lisa arrived pretty much on time after being ripped apart regarding her passport. Her current passport had expired. She'd managed to get a yearly passport which was just a piece of card folded into three equal parts and was obtained from a post office. Apparently, it's no longer available as it was withdrawn in 1996 due to security concerns. Presenting this sort of passport to Israeli security was cannon fodder. You can imagine their reaction to this sort of Mickey Mouse passport. She eventually emerged looking tired and excited but sounding a little apprehensive. This was understandable, given the fact that she had just been hauled over the proverbial Israeli coals. It was good to see her though... a familiar face.

We jumped onto the airport bus, which took us just past the Ramada Renaissance Hotel. I thought it best to tell Lisa about the hostel, that it wasn't a 5, or 4, or 3, or 2, or 1-star hostel, but a minus 5-star hostel. I tried to play down the fact that the resident bugs bit in a straight line, while simultaneously pointing to my lumpy forehead. It didn't go down very well as you can imagine, but I had to say something as I was remarkably close to looking like a Klingon. I'm not talking about the toilet type I might add! If you don't know what on God's earth I'm wittering on about, search up Klingons/*Star Trek*. Yeah, yeah, yeah, OK. You've rumbled me! I'm a closet Trekkie!

The cunning plan for the next two weeks was unravelled that night. Shabbat (the Jewish Holy Day) was on the horizon. It's pretty much equivalent to a Friday for Muslims and Sunday for Christians. Shabbat was happening in a couple of days and it was also the start of Rosh Hashanah (Jewish New Year) a couple of days after that. With all this going on, we decided to make our way to Jerusalem after Shabbat. There would be no Jewish shops open or buses running over the next few days and as Lisa only had two weeks, we didn't want to be stranded in Tel Aviv over Rosh Hashanah. We would then stay a few days in and around the Old City of Jerusalem and then travel north to Haifa, where we would catch the overnight ferry to Limassol in Cyprus. That was the plan.

During Shabbat we pottered about on the beach and generally did nothing in particular. In fact, we did lots of walking and talking. Tel Aviv really did shut down over Shabbat apart from the Arab and Christian shops. It seemed quite strict. I'd only seen this in action with the Orthodox Jewish community in Stamford Hill on a Friday night and Saturday, when no Jewish shops and businesses (that word again…UGH!) were open. In saying that, it was nice to see families and friends socialising after going to the synagogue, enjoying themselves and having quality time together.

JERUSALEM

The next day we jumped onto a local bus that took us to the Central Bus Station. We paid for two tickets on an Egged Bus, which was and still is the national bus service that takes you to other parts of the country. I thought it was an efficiently run service, similar to the role of the National Express coaches in the UK, and it was reasonably priced.

Jerusalem is situated inland, approximately a one-and-a-half-hour journey along what was once the old road. There is now a new direct road that takes less time. However, the old road was more interesting, especially as decimated tanks lay on the hills on the approach to Jerusalem, left over from the 1967 Six-Day War, when a number of Arab states attacked Israel. At the time, I knew something about the struggles on both sides (politically and religiously) prior to and after 1948, but not in any depth. Over the years, I've read quite a lot about the Middle East, taking into account both the Jewish and Palestinian viewpoints and interventions (both negative and positive) from other states including the British, American and Russian (USSR) governments. Having said this, it is an extremely emotive and sensitive issue.

We reached Jerusalem's Central Bus Station and the first thing we had to do was to find somewhere to stay. That really was the main objective when arriving at a new place. If that failed, a park bench, a secluded bush or a beach would be the next option but potentially a dangerous one. The first thing I noticed as we got off the bus were the hordes of people milling around the station as if there was no tomorrow. Rosh Hashanah and sundown were fast approaching. Everyone wanted to get to their respective families for the festivities. People were barging into us and offering no apologies. So, after a few similar incidents, the most natural thing to do was to reciprocate. The weird thing about it was that they didn't bat an eyelid. The whole behaviour was pretty much embedded. Then you had the people touting for business. No! No! No! Not that sort of business!

They were trying to drum up business to take red, sweaty-faced tourists to some kind of accommodation. The term 'some kind of accommodation' being the operative phrase. I'd been talking to fellow travellers in Tel Aviv about cheap but good places to stay in Jerusalem and they had mentioned the term 'some kind of accommodation'. They recommended a couple of hostels which they said were quite a way from the station. To be honest, I didn't fancy that. Being fully laden with rucksacks and walking around in the heat was not my idea of fun and I know it definitely wasn't Lisa's. We had various hairy individuals thrusting leaflets underneath our hooters and saying, "Hey, best food in Jerusalem. Very tasty!" or "Come to our hostel! Best hostel in Jerusalem! We have hot running water"; "We even have toilets..." etc. In all the excitement, they forgot to mention the phrase, "And if you're lucky we'll rip you off!" How could we resist an offer like that? Admittedly, it was hard to resist but somehow, we managed it.

Now having successfully navigated the vultures' den, we took a hostel flyer from someone outside the station. It said, 'Jasmine Hostel – a new hostel. Price includes breakfast' and it was four shekels a night! Pretty good, we thought, and it was only a ten-minute walk, or so the guy said. What more could we ask for? A ten-minute walk it wasn't... it was more like bloody half an hour and it was in the heat! The guy told us that when we got there, we were to give the manager the flyer which he had given us, with his name on it. Obviously, he was on commission. Somehow the slip of paper mysteriously disappeared. Hmm... I wonder how that happened... oh well! A ten-minute walk, he said, and he wanted his commission. I can honestly say that he wasn't getting it.

So, after being lightly fried en route, we found the Jasmine Hostel. At first, we weren't sure that it was the Jasmine Hostel until we saw a makeshift sign with the words, 'Jasmine Hostel' dripping in red paint. Someone should have told whoever painted these words on to the plywood to lay it flat and wait for the paint to dry before hanging it up. The sign looked like the opening credits to a horror film with blood dripping from each letter. Obviously, we hesitated!

Just like a film, out of the shadows, a stocky man with a shiny bald head, smoking a cigarette appeared and beckoned us in. It definitely tied in with the theme of the painted sign. All very dodgy! He looked us up and down, well not me so much, but Lisa. We kind of sheepishly asked if he had any rooms available. To be honest, we weren't sure if he even worked there. He showed us a room. It was literally a large room with nothing in it, apart from a basket in the corner, four walls, a floor, a door and a small window looking out onto the little courtyard where we had initially entered. The courtyard had a large, virginal, rectangular wooden table with a solitary ashtray and thatched chairs randomly littered around it. It was under a canopy that obviously kept the sun at bay. He went on to say that the price was four shekels per night (that was about £2.50 sterling), which included breakfast, tea or coffee and a hot shower. He said it was cheap because he had only been open about a week and that he was trying to find time to get beds etc. However, with Rosh Hashanah starting at sundown, the prospect of getting anything would be nigh on impossible. We said we would stay and we leant our rucksacks against the wall of our lavishly furnished room. I struck up some very good, one-sided conversations with my own little bit of concrete floor over the following few nights.

The owner introduced himself as David. Was he named after King David? Possibly. Possibly not! Who knows? Does anyone care? Anyway, he must have heard my first eccentric one-way dialogue with the floor when I mentioned how hard it was. The next thing we knew was that he turned up with two thin sleeping mats. A rather sympathetic touch I thought. Once we had settled in a bit and laid our sleeping bags out on the mats, David made us a coffee, which was unexpected but very welcome. We sat and chatted about what to see in Jerusalem and asked whether Lisa and I were a couple, to which we both simultaneously answered "yes", even though we weren't. It was probably the safest thing to say at the time. In reality, we were just good friends. Although I was initially suspicious, I was beginning have a better feeling about the place.

I asked about the basket in the corner. I jokingly asked if it was a laundry basket and whether he'd be doing our washing for us. He answered it by saying that it was Jasmine's. I answered, "Jasmine? Is that your daughter, wife, cousin, maid, mistress?" It was obviously a joke and he totally got it. I thought it was impressive especially as English was his second language. David started calling Jasmine. All of a sudden, this cute little brown puppy with large paws and floppy ears padded towards David from under a large-leafed plant. She was absolutely gorgeous.

After surgically parting with our shekels, we headed in the direction of the old walled city of Jerusalem. Personally, I was getting quite excited about seeing and touching the walls for the first time. I'd heard a lot about Jerusalem from my brother and my mum. My mum had been to Jerusalem countless times on pilgrimages and honestly, it seemed as if she knew it inside out. In my little munitions bag, I had a pocket-sized Bible. It was a *Good News* version of the New Testament. I took it to Israel as a point of reference. I was brought up as a Christian but not really a practising one. My mum, in her own sweet way, used to tell me brief biblical stories from the Old and New Testament.

My infant school in Crouch End also taught me these stories. I took part in the Nativity at the age of five and it was the first time I wore bright red tights, but it was not the last! Yes, I still remember it vividly, which I find truly incredible. Even now, I remember all the vibrant colours we were all wearing, the different coloured tinsel and the glittering Christmas tree. It was a totally magical moment for a five/six year old... ME!

The second and last time I wore tights was when I went to a Vicars and Tarts Party in Augsberg in Germany. I had met Lotte on a coach and we got on quite well. She invited me to stay with her for a few days, which I did. That was a huge risk on her part as she didn't really know me. I knew I would be totally respectful and no trouble but she didn't. Sorry, I'm being side-tracked as I remember this. Anyway, Lotte's friend dressed me up as a 'Tart', so to speak. They applied lashings of make-up which had to be removed using a hammer, chisel and a fire burning paint stripper. It couldn't be more over the top even if they'd tried. I looked hideous but it was funny. I was given a pair of red tights and putting them on was an education but taking them off was another matter. Having hairy legs probably didn't help. The amount of static electricity generated was amazing. It was a bit like pouring milk over a bowl of Rice Crispies and amplifying it through a 100-watt, Vox stack system. Incidentally, I wasn't just dressed in red tights and make up. I was given a black figure-hugging dress, along with three pairs of socks to give the impression that I was rather well-built. The most painful part about the whole experience were the very uncomfortable pair of high heels. How people wear those things is beyond me. They can't be very good for your legs and feet. Having said that, it was a bloody good party, as was my first ever Nativity. They were both very different for obvious reasons.

Back in Jerusalem, Lisa and I were both quite hungry. We strolled towards the stray wafting smells, of which there were loads. After we had had a bite to eat from a dodgy looking stall, we eventually saw the walls of the Old City as we walked towards them. This was a genuinely magnificent and majestic sight. Jerusalem's original Old City is believed to go back more than three thousand years and these particular walls must have seen some action over the years. Jerusalem has been occupied by many groups including the Egyptians, Persians, Greeks, Romans, Crusaders and the Ottomans, which must have given the Old City something to think about throughout its turbulent existence.

We were trying to find one of the twelve gates to enter the Old City. Eight gates are open and four are sealed. We walked along the perimeter of the walls with its overhead ramparts until we came to Jaffa Gate, which is in between the Christian and the Armenian Quarters. At the time, I assumed that the gate was named Jaffa Gate because it was in the direction of Jaffa. I applied the same logic to Damascus Gate when I eventually got there.

Just before entering the gate, we were stopped by a young lady with tight, curly, ginger, shoulder-length hair called Honey. She just started chatting away with us about nothing in particular at first. It transpired after a few minutes that she belonged to a group called *Jews for Jesus*. They promoted Messianic Judaism, which was a new Christian religious movement. As it happened, she wasn't trying to sell us anything materialistic as we first thought but something spiritual. Before the conversation became too deep, we politely gave our apologies and moved on. As we left and before we could break into a Miranda type of canter, she gave us a tiny book. It was made of card and was about two centimetres square. Amazingly, I still have it! I know it sounds bizarre but it's something that I have strangely treasured. I occasionally look at it remembering this scene. However, this was not the last I would see of her.

We quickly walked through Jaffa Gate and in front of us, we were greeted by a sea of colour and muffled noises. It was great! We headed towards a wasps' nest of people mingling around a jar of honey. People kept coming and going from what looked like a dark hole. Obviously, it wasn't a hole. It was the brightness of the sun blocking out much of the visual clarity. We went down a few steps and approached the mouth of the beast. We heard the dull noise increase and then suddenly there was an ocean of people milling around the shop stalls, which were selling anything and everything from clothes, to jewellery, to food and funnily enough, the shop owners' siblings and children. It was just fantastic – a bit like the markets in Tel Aviv, but in this case, they were very much more tightly packed together giving the impression of a very busy train station back home during rush hour. From a security point of view it seemed a tad dodgy but we went in all the same. It reminded me a little bit of Notting Hill Carnival in that respect. Incidentally, the film *Notting Hill* is one of my favourite films. It's definitely a film to watch!

This particular place that we stumbled across was obviously part of the Christian Quarter as it was full of crucifixes, charcoal burners, frankincense etc. Try and visualise the scene. In amongst all this were the shop owners selling souvenirs at what they called cheap prices, but knowing full well that they were overpriced. You could hear the haggling going on. It was absolutely fascinating. I couldn't help watching and listening to the banter, which was an integral part of the haggling process. It reminds me of a great haggling scene in Monty Python's *Life of Brian*. If you've seen the film, you'll know what I'm talking about. If you haven't, then you seriously need to watch it. Such a brilliant film! They pretty much ridicule everything. There are no taboos. As a result, the Church was not happy. John Cleese and Michael Palin were invited to go on a late-night TV programme on BBC2 to discuss the film with the Bishop of Southwark and Malcolm Muggeridge, who was a born-again Christian. The debate was described as 'one of TV's all-time ding-dongs'. If you want to watch the debate, it's on You Tube.

As we walked around taking everything in, we were approached by various shop owners. Well, to be honest, it was mainly Lisa who was the focus. Her hair at the time was quite a light shade, which is a bit of magnet in those parts. We would hear things like "Pretty lady...come, come... I have many lovely things for you. I have beautiful earrings and necklaces. My brothers, my uncles, my friends are all here... are you married? Would you like to meet them?" They asked the usual questions like "Where are you from?" "London", we'd say to which they would reply, "Ah yes, I have a friend in London". I bet they have a friend in every city and in every country in the world! The whole thing was quite funny really and we spent the remaining part of the day just walking round and making sure we didn't get lost. Initially, it seemed very easy to get lost in the Old City as there were so many nooks and crannies to explore, but as time went on, we got used to it.

At some point we had crossed into the Jewish Quarter. The only way that we had realised this was mainly due to the fact that most signs were in Hebrew. We stumbled across a large open area with a massive wall. We noticed that the security was stepped up quite considerably in and around this area, which was the Western Wall, also known as the Wailing Wall. It's a sacred place of prayer and pilgrimage for the Jewish people. It is the only remaining part of the wall surrounding Temple Mount, the site of the First and Second Temples of Jerusalem. The First Temple was destroyed by the Babylonians in 587-586 BC and the Second Temple was destroyed by the Romans in 70 AD. On the site of Temple Mount, in place of the First and Second Temples, stand two important Islamic structures. The first one, Al-Haram al-Sharif, is also known as the Dome of the Rock. The dome is gold-coloured. You can't miss it, especially if you look at an aerial view of Jerusalem. Al-Aqsa Mosque is the other building on Temple Mount. The site has been a bone of contention for years between the Jewish and Muslim communities.

From a distance, the Western Wall didn't seem that big but as we drew nearer you could see how big it was. It was absolutely enormous. Men and women were separated. Men were on the left side of the wall and women on the right, so Lisa and I went into our designated areas. After I donned my paper kippah (worn on the head as a sign of respect and fear of God), the first thing I noticed was the size of the limestone blocks that made up the Western Wall. They were massive! I'm always in awe of these ancient structures, especially as they were built a good few thousand years ago without the technology and equipment that we have now.

In between each block, prayers to God had been written on small slips of paper and inserted into the crevices. Apparently, the thousands of slips of paper in the crevices are collected and buried on Jerusalem's Mount of Olives twice a year without being looked at. This is done in order to create space for future slips of paper. Many people would alternatively close their eyes, lean forward and with their foreheads touching the wall. They would then whisper their prayers to God and kiss the wall. Others were rocking from their waist upwards and reading from what I assumed was the Torah. On the right-hand side of the wall, the women were praying. They would also have to cover their heads with either a scarf or a hat as opposed to a kippah.

Seeing as I was at the wall, I left a little note in one of the many crevices but what I wrote in it was between me and God. Lisa did the same. I didn't ask her what she wrote. That was also between herself and God. One of the other things that intrigued me was a gated passage to the left of the Western Wall which was under a cover. There were men in this narrow corridor praying and rocking at the same time. I didn't go in this time. I saved the experience for a later date. After sitting around and watching for a little while, Lisa and I left the Western Wall and decided to head back to the hostel.

The sun was beginning to set when we reached the hostel. I was looking forward to having another chat with my new friend the concrete floor, who funnily enough, never ever answered. While we were out, three Australian girls and a Spanish guy had booked in and had their rucksacks in the same well-furnished room as us. We started chatting about all the usual things that travellers chat about, such as places they had visited, food, underwear, why more men don't wear high heels and why thongs in Australia are Britain's equivalent to flip-flops! Now, I have to say, that it was a very informative discussion which verged very much on the ridiculous. It was most enjoyable! We chatted and drank tea and coffee most of the night. We eventually decided to get a good night's sleep given the luxurious bedding we had. They were in the same predicament as us but they came prepared with decent ground mats. You can always count on the Aussies. Well, sort of!

We had all decided to hang out together and go to Jericho the next day, which was a bus ride away. As it was the Jewish New Year the next day, nothing would be open or running. However, the Arab shops and services would be open as usual. Well, that was the plan. Anyway, we went to our respective sleeping bags. I climbed into mine with the clothes I had been wearing for the last two days thinking that I must change tomorrow, when Lisa gave out a muted scream of shock mixed in with, "What the fuck is that?!" Something in her sleeping bag was moving. She was just about to unzip her bag when a small dog-like head appeared and there she was; Jasmine the puppy. We all gushed over her saying how cute she was. Well, as cute as Jasmine was, our second encounter was tinged with freshly produced puppy piss. Now that was not so cute! It was a pain in the proverbial arse to say the least for Lisa and as it also turned out, for me as well.

While all this commotion was going on, David came bounding out of his room kitted out with his flak jacket, no trousers, and a pair of big, black twenty-one holed, steel toe-capped army issue boots. He was holding a machine gun in one hand and a grenade in the other with the pin in his mouth, while on his back, there was a scantily clad blow-up doll hanging on for dear life. As he watched the situation manically unfold, he informed us that Jasmine wasn't totally housetrained yet and that it was something he'd forgotten to tell us. No! Really? I would never have guessed! David apologised profusely and quickly washed Lisa's sleeping bag and hung it out to dry overnight. I ended up handing over my sleeping bag to Lisa and I slept with a blanket with Jasmine lying across my face. Just to remind you and before your minds start racing, Jasmine was a puppy...

The rosy fingers of dawn emerged with no overnight incidents, which was helpful. It seemed that we'd all slept well and that we were ready for our DIY jaunt to Jericho. After our 'all-inclusive breakfast', we all made our way to the Arab bus station, which was situated outside the Old City walls at a place called Skull Hill. This was not far from Damascus Gate. If you looked above all the retro buses you could see why it was called Skull Hill. It actually resembled a skull... we could see what looked like the eye sockets and a space which could have been a nose.

Biblically, according to *Luke 23:33*, Jesus was crucified at a place called 'The Skull', which in Hebrew apparently translates into Golgotha. Some people believe that this is the true site of Jesus' crucifixion and next to it is the Garden Tomb (Jesus' tomb). Others believe that the site of Golgotha, or Calvary as it's also called, is traditionally situated inside the Church of the Holy Sepulchre. It is said that Queen Helena, the mother of Constantine the Great, identified the crucifixion site and the Tomb of Jesus in 325 AD (about 300 years later) and consequently built the Church of the Holy Sepulchre around this area, proclaiming it the true site. The church is inside the Old City walls.

Jericho is a small Palestinian city situated on the West Bank and is east of Jerusalem. It's mentioned in the Old Testament. Biblically, it is well known for the battle that took place. As the story goes, the walls of Jericho fell after the Israelites walked around them carrying the Ark of Covenant. They walked around them once a day for six days and then on the seventh day, they walked around it seven times in their quest to conquer the Land of Canaan.

We approached Jericho in an old, knackered and dusty bus. It was so hot that it had holes in the floor for extra ventilation or alternatively, to put your legs through to help it go faster or even help it to go uphill. The bus eventually stopped and everyone got out but there wasn't much going on in our immediate vicinity apart from more buses and stalls of food. Surely this couldn't be Jericho? There was nothing there! We had it on good authority that the city was a little further on and we were persuaded to hire bicycles for the day to cycle further on. The bikes had definitely seen better days. They didn't exactly fill us with confidence and guess what? It was midday and as the saying goes, 'Only mad dogs and Englishman are out in the midday sun'. In our case it was three Aussies, one Spaniard, one English woman and a Greek out in the midday sun. This was coupled with us riding a collection of rickety old road bikes, armed with a rather large water melon which was bought at one of the many stalls. On a positive note, the brakes on all the bikes actually worked, which was a miracle in itself. Mind you, the chain often came off one of the Aussie girls' bikes.

We were all getting hot and embarrassingly sweaty as we cycled, so we decided to stop by a coachload of people milling around a rather large, old-looking tree. It occurred to me that we could compare our sweaty patches with theirs. Probably not a good idea! Apparently, this was the Tree of Zacchaeus, who is said to have climbed this particular tree to see Jesus, who was on his way to Jerusalem. After they had left, we found some shade and dissected the water melon with my Swiss Army knife. We pretty much devoured the whole thing. It was very refreshing but extremely sweet and sticky, which ultimately attracted flies, mad dogs and the inevitable Englishman! It was around mid-afternoon, so we decided to head back as we couldn't find the main part of the city. How useless were we? Very useless! In fact, we were worse than useless! Feeling tired, hard done by and very sticky, we headed back to Jerusalem in another one of those Flintstone-styled buses.

Once back in Jerusalem and after being watered and fed, we decided to go to the Mount of Olives, where it is said that Jesus ascended to Heaven. We also pottered around the Garden of Gethsemane which is pretty much at the bottom of the Mount of Olives where Jesus was arrested. Apparently, the Mount of Olives is named after the fact that it once had olive groves lining it. Obviously! For three thousand years the mount has been a Jewish cemetery and is still used today for that purpose. I didn't know it at the time, but Oskar Schindler is buried on Mount Zion, which faces the Mount of Olives across the Kidron Valley. Schindler was a German businessman who rescued 1,200 Jews from the Nazis in World War 2.

During the time that we were there, I was trying to imagine the scene back in the day when Jesus was arrested. In fact, I was trying to picture what Jerusalem was like during that time. I mentioned this to one of the Australian girls. Her name was Beth and she was by far the most outgoing of the three and the shortest! They reminded me of Russian dolls in that they would easily fit inside each other. That's not an image I would want to encourage. They were very visibly different in their height.

As I was saying, I mentioned to Beth that I was trying to imagine what it was like back in the days of Jesus and the Romans. As a result, we had quite a long on-going discussion about it. It transpired that she was a practising Christian and she found it amazing that she was walking on the same land that Jesus possibly walked on. That included the land around these hills and Jerusalem. I suppose a lot of Christians would think something similar. She also said that they were going to follow the Twelve Stations of the Cross where Jesus walked with the cross. The First Station was where he was condemned to death. The Second Station was where Jesus took up the cross. The Third Station was where Jesus fell for the first time and so on. I have to admit that this didn't really appeal to me. We talked quite a bit that day. We touched on the subject of Kylie Minogue, Jason Donovan, and the *Neighbours* soap. I mentioned that I had the hots for Jane Harris (that's her character name and was commonly known as *Plain Jane*). We jokingly spoke about how *Neighbours* had impacted on our lives and how we could produce some kind of religious book based on the teaching of the *Neighbours* script and characters. The whole thing spiralled into so much nonsense that I found it liberating that someone was playing along with it. In all honesty, what else would I talk to an Aussie about? To be fair, we did have some deep conversations. It was then that she asked me if Lisa and I were an item. I replied by saying we were siblings but had different fathers. She didn't believe me. I said that we were just good friends and I told her that I was out for the long haul and that Lisa was visiting and having a break from London for a couple of weeks.

The next day we all decided to go to Bethlehem; Jesus' birthplace. Bethlehem is south of Jerusalem and once again we took the bus from the Arab bus station at Skull Hill. Bethlehem is another Palestinian town and my first impression was that it was quite run-down and dusty. We asked the bus driver where the Church of the Nativity was and he pointed us in the right direction. I was not sure what to expect but it certainly wasn't what I saw. Of course, I expected a modest-sized church of sorts but not on this scale. It wasn't just huge. It was bloody enormous, and somewhere in there was Jesus' birthplace. This is no exaggeration. This place was massive... I was shocked!

Apparently, Queen Helena had had a hand in identifying Jesus' birthplace and she ordered a church to be built above the cave where the stable would have possibly been situated. Emperor Constantine approved the site in AD 335. This is apparently the traditional view of what happened. The site came to be known as the Church of the Nativity and it is still called that to this day. I remember thinking at the time that it must be an incredible place to visit during the Christmas period. These days the Church of the Nativity is owned by the Greek Orthodox, Armenian Apostolic and the Roman Catholic churches.

We entered the building through a small stone doorway and I personally was in awe of the place. The first things I noticed were the floor and the columns on either side as we walked along. The floor was made up of huge rectangular-shaped stone slabs that seemed to have been polished. They weren't polished. It's just were people had walked over the years. There was also what looked like an avenue of columns which was equally as impressive. It kind of resembled an avenue of trees leading up to the entrance of a stately home. We all wandered around looking at various bits and pieces until we came to a series of stone steps leading through to another doorway. This led to some more steps descending into what I suppose was the grotto – the place where Jesus was supposedly born. I wouldn't say that I was overcome with emotion – far from it, but I felt something special about being there. I had a feeling of immense peace in what was quite a chaotic environment. I say chaotic because lots of other people in the grotto were quite disrespectful. They were very loud given that this place is quite important and sacred. Maybe it was just these particular tourists... hopefully it was. Most of the commotion was centred around the traditional place of Jesus' birth, which was pretty much a silver star placed on the floor. People wanted to see it and touch it, which is a perfectly natural thing to do, but in doing so, they were unintentionally pushing others. We waited until they were militarily marched out, with their arms tied behind their backs and duck tape slapped across their mouths by their visibly embarrassed guides.

Once they had left, we had a peaceful look around without all the pushing and shoving. Before we knew it, another collection of individuals had quietly descended, so we decided to leave the grotto. It's a good job that we left when we did as there were hordes of people waiting to go in. At least we had a couple of minutes' worth of silence while being there. I still couldn't get over the size of the place, though. As a reward for tortuously dodging and surviving all the organised tourist tours with their guides, who by the way were holding multi-coloured umbrellas, we decided to satisfy our rumbling tums with falafels. The interesting thing about having falafels in different places is that they are all subtly different in their own way. I suppose it boils down to who is making them. Maybe it's a way of putting their own mark on them. It's quite good comparing them, though!

The first time I'd tried Arabic coffee was in Bethlehem. It's very much like Greek and Turkish coffee but they use crushed cardamom seeds, which sends it up to another level. It's bliss! The coffee reminded me of a time when I was at BT and working with an engineer called Dennis. He also went under the guise of Jazz. We called him Jazz simply because he loved jazz music and the fact that one of his front teeth was made of gold and he looked very cool for an older gent. He was definitely a bit of a dude.

We were on residential duties for the day and ended up in Haringey, which at the time had a huge Greek Cypriot community. When we had finished the allocated work in the house, we were invited to have a Greek coffee. The lovely old lady whose house it was brought out the coffee with a whole load of savoury goodies and we chatted for around twenty minutes about the usual things old ladies talk about. She talked about her family, showed us photos, etc. We were doing our community relations bit, which was actually part of our job at the time. Anyway, once we'd finished our coffee and nibbles, we said that we had to go to the next job and promptly left. We climbed into our bright yellow van and the old lady waved us off as if we were going off to war. Jazz turned to me and said, "How can anyone drink that stuff? It's foul". I have to say that the language he used was rather more colourful. The words sounded similar to "shucking fit". Hopefully, you're able to work that one out. Otherwise, you may want to ask an irresponsible adult! Anyway, it turned out that he ended up drinking and chewing the coffee sludge at the bottom of the cup. It's something that you don't do! It's disgusting. Looking back, maybe I should have told him about the sludge.

So, regarding the coffee in Bethlehem, Lisa and one of the Aussie girls also ordered an Arabic coffee, so I warned them that once they get to the sludge to stop, don't pass go and do not collect 200 shekels! It was at this point that we decided to go to the Church of the Holy Sepulchre back in Jerusalem. The logic behind this was that we'd seen Jesus' traditional birthplace so now we wanted to go and see the traditional place of Jesus' crucifixion.

Once inside Jerusalem's Old City, we made our way to the Church of the Holy Sepulchre, and apart from the throngs of people in the courtyard, you wouldn't have known it was there. It wasn't massively obvious. We knew we were in the right area because there were lots of shops selling crucifixes and Jesus-type things.

Excitedly, we just walked around and looked at everything. There was so much to see. We came to what looked like a little church within the church where a long queue had formed. We were told that this was the Tomb of Jesus after he was taken down from the cross and then resurrected. There was no chaos here… it was quite orderly. The tomb wasn't very big so I was glad it was a one person in and one person out policy. Once inside the tomb, I felt at peace again. It might have something to do with the fact that I was alone, but peaceful, nevertheless. It was lit up with candles and had some icons hanging on the walls. The place where Jesus was laid on was a bed of stone. To protect it, a slab of marble was laid over the top. You could see where people had touched the marble, just as I had. Over the years, it has been partly worn away. I've lost count of how many times my mum had been on her pilgrimages, which had been organised through the church. She would always go around the time of the Orthodox Easter, where she and hundreds of others would be waiting for the holy light. It's believed that a blue light rises from Jesus' stone slab within his tomb. It's claimed that unlit oil lamps and candles ignite spontaneously. My mum would often talk about this.

From Jesus' tomb, we walked through the church over to where Jesus was crucified. This was known as Calvary. There have been many debates as to where Jesus was crucified. The Bible mentions 'the place of the skull', which is where the Arab bus station is. It is said that around a decade after Jesus' crucifixion, another wall was built to encompass the area of his crucifixion, burial and resurrection. This apparently validates the Church of the Holy Sepulchre's location within the current walls of the Old City. I have to say it was most certainly an experience, as was visiting Jesus' birthplace. I'm glad I experienced both on the same day.

It was very late afternoon. Lisa and I went for a walk while the others went back to the hostel. We arranged to go out later to eat when we got back. While we were out, we fell upon lots of Orthodox Jews in the street, shaking hands. We assumed they were wishing each other a Happy New Year. We kind of got into it as well and wished people a Happy New Year, like anyone would do. But no, that wasn't the case for us! As we walked, taking everything in, people avoided us, not looking at us or acknowledging us. I suppose not being acknowledged is an acknowledgement in itself. As we walked, spaces would open up around us. It was like Moses and the parting of the Red Sea. A path opened out in front of us! Were we modern-day lepers? They wouldn't come anywhere near us. We both sensed an air of hostility. It was becoming rapidly evident.

Orthodox Jews are easily identifiable by what they wear. It's a kind of religious uniform. The men wear black hats, black coats, white shirts, black trousers, black shoes, long sprawling beards and shawls, etc. Very much like my fellow passenger on the outward flight. There did seem to be some variation in the dress code, though. Some men wore what looked like coats with majestically embroidered and coloured designs. Whether they were elders of some sort, I couldn't really tell you. However, the whole scene was a mixture of wonder and anticipation. The women also had a religious 'uniform' code to follow like the men. They seemed to be wearing wigs. These would mainly be the Orthodox women. According to the Talmud (which in essence is a recorded text of debates by Rabbis in the 2nd - 5th century on the teaching of the Torah) the uncovered hair of a woman is equivalent to physical nudity; hence, the wigs, hats and headscarves. You can usually tell if people are wearing wigs. Something about wigs look different but that's not always the case. In addition to the head-gear, they wore blouses, jumpers, cardigans, long skirts with thick tights and flat shoes. They mainly dressed in dark colours, not necessarily black like the men. I suppose the main objective for both men and women is that in the eyes of God, all parts of their bodies are covered. I've obviously given you a simplified accountant regarding the dress code, otherwise I would have gone on about it for ages. If you're interested, do take the time to read-up about it… it's fascinating.

Anyway, as I was saying, they didn't want us there… that much was clear. Out of respect for them and our safety, Lisa and I decided to leave the area. We headed back to the hostel, where we arranged to meet the other four and then head off for some nutritional sustenance!

When we got back to the hostel, David asked us if we'd had a good day and we said that we had. As we spoke about what just happened, the others came into the courtyard and listened. David told us that it was the end of Rosh Hashanah and that people in some areas would greet others and shake hands, etc. He informed us that unfortunately we had drifted in the Mea She'arim neighbourhood, who were not averse to a spot of stoning. He looked at what we were wearing and said that we were lucky not to be stoned.

"You don't go to that place looking like that!" were his words. "It's offensive to them!"

I'm going to go off piste for a few sentences so please bear with me! If you haven't seen the stoning scene in Monty Python's *Life of Brian*, then please take a break and watch it. It's a must. It's bloody funny! To be perfectly honest, we were not exactly appropriately dressed for *First Contact*, which incidentally is a great *Star Trek* film involving the Borg. I love the Borg. They're scary but such a great concept.

We both wore shorts and T-shirts. However, Lisa's top was an off-the-shoulder number which probably didn't go down too well, and before you say anything, yes, we were always appropriately dressed for places of worship. We covered up! Only this time we didn't expect it. Having said that, we did have thin shawls in our bags from earlier but it didn't occur to us that we should cover ourselves up with them.

So, while we digested what could have happened, we teamed up with our own personal mini United Nations unit and headed into the Old City. The sun had set for the night and it was already dark. We had been warned not to go into the Old City during these times. Hey, what could go wrong, I may well hear you ask? It's a long story, but I'll tell you! Are you seated comfortably? Are you sure? That's good. Then I'll begin.

Once upon a time, there were six tourists who were advised not to go into the Old City when it was dark but they foolishly did…

Initially, it was OK around the Jewish Quarter, as it was busy due to the end of Rosh Hashanah. We went further in and it was like a ghost town. The shops had shut and darkness had set in, making it uncomfortable and creepy but strangely calming at the same time. All the while, as we were walking and nattering, I was thinking that this was not good. It was eerily quiet and the only thing you could hear were our voices and our collective footsteps echoing along the streets. The whole place was badly lit so we could not see too far into the distance. We then realised that we had crossed quarters and were in the Arab Quarter. We recognised this purely from the Arabic writing everywhere. The whole point about the evening was to find some food, which was turning out to be a bit sparse.

We eventually found a café that seemed in need of a deep clean and a spot of paint. There were two young guys sitting inside and chatting. They soon stopped when they saw us. As it was the only place with the lights on and the shutters up, we asked if it was open. I couldn't quite work out whether they were in the process of closing the café as they were a bit off with us. Were they annoyed that we had turned up and interrupted their conversation or were they just naturally miserable bastards? In my opinion, it was probably the latter! One of them, a short, slim and rather sweaty individual began to say that they were about to close. That was the point at which we should have turned around and gradually walked away and then legged it. Meanwhile, the other guy, who was tall, slim and equally sweaty, beckoned us in and with a rather unfriendly smile, told us to ignore what his friend had just said.

Now this is the scene... we'd sat down at a large round table and ordered food and drinks. In hindsight, we felt that we were very fortunate that the drinks had not been laced with anything. Anyway, back to the original timeframe. Both guys were looking at all of us and were whispering. Imagine the situation, four girls and two blokes who probably wouldn't be able to fight their way out of a paper bag, all ramming the food down their throats, as if they hadn't eaten for weeks. Happy with the speed that we had downed the food, we asked for the bill. We settled up and attempted to get the hell out of there as quickly as it was humanly possible. The vibes were not good. The taller of the two asked us what the hurry was and insisted that we should have a chat so that they could practise their English. He then offered us drinks on the house. We reluctantly agreed but we all knew it was a bad idea because we all exchanged panic-stricken glances. We asked for teas and coffees. The taller guy brought them over and he started asking us where we were from.

As he spoke you could hear the agitation in his voice. By this time, he was sporting a makeshift carving knife, which had the handle taped up with countless strips of well-thumbed red electrical insulation tape, which was beginning to curl up. The smaller guy stood behind the serving counter, just observing. The taller guy started with the Australian girls and he correctly guessed their nationality. Meanwhile, he was touching their upper arms and shoulders with his free hand. At that point the girls were protesting and he stopped. He then turned to Lisa and she said that she was English – he didn't try anything on with her. He then turned to our Spanish friend. He asked where he was from and he replied by saying, "Spain". At this point our new friend with the knife mimicked him and said "Spain!" and added, "You are a nothing race" which really was a WHOA moment. Did I really hear right? Our Spanish friend, who was a gentle soul, didn't do or say anything for obvious reasons. He just looked at our friendly knife bearer. The gloves were definitely starting to slip off his hands now, metaphorically speaking. He then rounded on me and thinking about it, he purposely left me till last. He then said to me in a menacingly manner,

"And you are... Israeli". That is when I thought the shit was going to hit the fan big time and in no uncertain terms... if it hadn't done so already.

So, let's stop it there for the moment and look at the facts:

- We were warned not to go into the Old City at night.

- It was dark and everything was shut.

- No one knew that we were wandering around the Old City alone.

- There was a madman with a makeshift carving knife.

- And well, yes, I looked Israeli. I was tanned, had short hair, had a munitions bag and I was starting to blend in quite well.

Putting it mildly, things were not going too well! With all that said I tried to explain to him that my parents were Greek and that I was a Greek god! I told him that I lived in the UK supporting twenty-eight kids from eleven different mothers and we all lived harmoniously in a sky-blue 1973 Volkswagen caravanette, with no catalytic converter! He still didn't believe me. He still thought that I was an Israeli who was in the Arab Quarter, in the dark and no one else around except for five tourists. I could go missing! We could all go missing! That's what was going through my mind at that moment. Maybe that's what was going through his mind as well. Or maybe he was playing and if he was, then I can tell you that it was not a very pleasant game.

After giving me a rather hard stare, as if he was trying to read my panic-ridden beads of sweat, he asked me a question.

"Do you like baklava?"

Of course I like baklava. I'm of ethnic Greek origin and I was weaned on the stuff! What a stupid question, but I obviously wasn't going to challenge his mental abilities, especially when he was spit-polishing his knife with an old manky cloth. So, I replied by saying,

"Nope... I'm allergic to nuts!"

Just for your information I'm not allergic to nuts. I'm just allergic to nutters like him. He completely ignored my allergy comment and answered by saying,

"You must try some, my mother made it. She will be offended if you don't have some... and so will I!"

Who was I to argue? He had the knife. He then went to the back of the shop and produced six small pieces of baklava. We should have made a run for it there and then but again, we didn't. Why didn't we run? Why did we even go into the cafe? This was turning out to be a bit of a disturbing habit. The others quickly ate their baklava, which was rhombus or diamond-shaped, depending on how you positioned it in front of you.

Before I could take my slab of filo pastry, syrup and nuts he said, "No my friend, I will feed you." Wow! What an offer! Did I get to lie on some kind of Roman couch and get fed grapes at the same time? Who was I to refuse a maniac brandishing one of the favourite tools of his trade? So, I gulped and out came a very meek "OK!" He took the delightfully shaped pastry, told me to open my mouth, which I reluctantly did and he delicately placed it in my mouth. He then showed me his middle finger and asked:

"Do you know what this means?"

I grudgingly nodded, fully aware of what he was going to do. He proceeded to push the baklava into my mouth with his middle finger accompanied with:

"This is for you, my Israeli friend!"

From where I was sitting, I could see the smaller guy and he had a look of concern plastered all over his face, as did everyone else sat around the table. Given what had just happened, I have to say that it was a very tasty baklava! Very tasty indeed!

Once I had eaten it, I said, "Give my compliments to your mum, it was delicious. You must be very proud of her!"

Thinking back, I really hoped he had washed his hands but I very much doubt it! It probably added to the texture and the taste.

So that was that! He said he had to shut the shop and that we should go. Such is the mercy of gods, kings, lions and psychopaths brandishing glistening carving knives! We did just as he advised. We buggered off and I might add that we didn't have to be asked twice. It was a quick getaway given that the Aussie girls were wearing flip-flops. They're not exactly built for making quick getaways. I'm talking about the flip-flops, not the Aussies! Through the dark and deserted alleyways, we kept looking behind us just in case we were being followed. In fact, we looked in every direction possible until with much relief, we were out of the Old City.

I must say, that it was an interesting encounter! We all agreed that we should have heeded the warnings but for some reason we didn't. Still, when all is said and done, this was something we could tell our children as a bedtime story. It was definitely an eventful few hours for both Lisa and I. From being potentially stoned by Orthodox Jews to being insulted and abused at knifepoint by a psychotic café owner. It couldn't have gone better even if we'd tried! It was surprising that we all slept well that night.

The next day, we all just took it easy and pottered about in the Old City. I wanted to go the Yadva Shem, the Holocaust Museum, but it was the last day before we were due to go Haifa. It's in the north of Israel and we were to catch the overnight ferry to Cyprus. I suppose I could always go to Yadva Shem another time, which I did. There really was no rush. I had all the time in the world as long as I stayed away from psychos wielding maternally baked baklavas and makeshift carving knives.

In the light of day, the Old City felt a lot safer than the previous night. There were loads of people milling around this time. We kept away from last night's salubrious eatery, although I was entertaining the idea of taking a well-oiled tank division to sample the psycho's mother's baklava. Even if we could weave a few tanks through the Old City, there was probably no way we could have found it even if we tried. We didn't even know what the café was called. It now seemed that our little adventure was in the back and beyond, in last night's shadows. Just as well really!

Anyway, we spent the day just dossing in shops and cafés, like you do! We did a little bit of haggling but that was about it. That morning, the Spanish guy left the hostel to go Eilat on the Red Sea, so we were now down to five... definitely not what Enid Blyton would have had in mind. Beth and I spent a good amount of that day talking and by the end of it she'd invited me to Adelaide and I invited her back to London. I decided that I would not exchange addresses with everyone I met, just a select few that I felt comfortable with. You didn't know who or what you were going to end up with on your doorstep.

Talking about people ending up on your doorstep, my brother once had two German girls called Andrea and Nina from Munich staying with us for a few days. Taking into account that I was only fifteen at the time, it was like Christmas coming early for me. They had no inhibitions about how they presented themselves. It was what a red-blooded teenager's dreams were made of. It was absolutely fantastic! I'm going to have to keep to an appropriate collection of words to describe what I was experiencing. In other words, a nod is as good as a wink.

One morning I'd got up early to get a quick pubescent peek by knocking on their door, which was our front room door. I used the pretence of asking them if they wanted a tea, coffee and something to nibble on like toast or a young teenager. I very quickly made them a coffee. I sat with them and spent the next half an hour or so chatting, getting an eyeful and changing my bib... twice! Who wouldn't? I don't mean the bib bit. They were scantily dressed in their sleeping bags and I have to say that I was more than happy. My mum, on the other hand, was a bit more conservative about how they were dressed. She couldn't believe how my brother even convinced her to agree for them to stay with us. How he managed it was a complete mystery to me. My mum could be a tough cookie to crack. Either way, I was not one to complain! In fact, I had to stop myself from hugging my brother profusely and repeatedly saying, "Thank-you! Thank-You! Thank-You!" and "You don't know how much I appreciate all this!", as if it was all meant for my benefit. I know it's over the top but I was only fifteen and very, very, very grateful! Did I mention that I was grateful?

Sorry! I digress... again! The following day we all said our goodbyes. The girls were going to Tel Aviv to catch a plane to Izmir in Turkey. In a way we kind of grew close in a very short space of time, which is something that happens. You either get on or you kill each other. From my viewpoint, I felt a little sad that I wouldn't see them again unless I went to the land of Aus, but that's how it was and I accepted that. We had our plans and they had theirs.

We caught a bus to the Port of Hafia and arrived mid-afternoon armed with our return ferry tickets. We both grabbed a falafel pitta heaped with a horrendous amount of salad that once again put Mount Kilimanjaro to shame. We also bought some drinks for our evening meal, which we would have on the boat and then made our way through the dreaded Israeli security checkpoints. Apart from sniffing the air and eventually massaging our deck-class feast, security asked us the same questions as before and searched our bags. They didn't really pay too much attention to Lisa's make-do passport and asked us what we did while in Israel. They didn't seem as thorough as when we'd both entered the country. They were probably happy to get rid of us!

We made our way onto the ferry, which incidentally was called the *F/B Vergina*. I nearly wet myself. I had this rapidly developing image unfolding in my head, that our fellow seafarers would be rolling around on the floor, laughing so much they'd be foaming at the mouth, when the Captain welcomed everyone onto his vessel...*The Vergina*. I was surprised that no one batted an eyelid. Although the spelling was different, I did find it hugely entertaining. It's the little abstract things in life that do it for me!

CYPRUS

Once we were aboard, we (the scruffy ones) were directed to the rear of the ferry. The back of the boat was an open-top lower deck which was covered with a green layer of moderately thick carpet for want of a better word. I actually expected a hard and rusty metallic floor, so I was pleasantly surprised. We'd claimed our spot for the journey and laid out our sleeping bags, making sure there were no puppies around to deposit their goods. We were situated on one of the internal perimeter walls of the ferry and watched as more cheapskate travellers like ourselves were claiming their spots. I'm glad we arrived early as the perimeter spots were the first to go, closely followed by the middle area, which eventually resembled a human warehouse scene. It was total carnage! There were arms, legs and rucksacks everywhere.

We finally set off on our twelve-hour and one-hundred-and-seventy-mile overnight journey across the Mediterranean Sea. I felt quite excited that we'd be sleeping under the stars, on a boat and in the middle of nowhere. I was just hoping that it wasn't going to rain! We chugged along and watched Haifa disappear into the distance. To keep us company, we saw seagulls hovering behind the boat looking for any scraps of food which had been chucked overboard. We also saw dolphins swimming alongside us, which is something I did not expect to see. It was a beautiful sight. After a couple of hours, the sun was beginning to set and I can only say that it was truly stunning. We live in such a naturally beautiful world that some of us don't appreciate enough, if at all. Out there in the middle of the sea, you have no choice but to appreciate it. Watching the sun gradually setting always amazes me. It's as if the sun drops behind the horizon, while at the same time, pulling down the remainder of the day with its warm colours to keep it company. It then magically reveals its tiny winking specks of light in the dark night sky. Only then do you realise that you are totally alone in this vast expanse of water. It was slightly frightening and at the same time, an exhilarating moment for me.

Lisa and I tucked into the food we'd bought earlier and literally just settled in for the night while talking to a few people. The toilets were interesting. They were initially clean but as time happily ticked away, their state invaded all our senses except for our sense of touch. (You really did not want to touch any of that stuff. YUK!) How blokes can't piss in a straight line into a large oval-shaped bowl is beyond me. As it happens, Lisa came back with a similar description. We spoke about women hovering over the toilet so that they don't sit on a soiled toilet seat just to avoid catching anything. Some people just don't care how they leave things. It's common courtesy to clean up after ourselves and not leave it to others! I was hoping the toilet would be cleaned by the morning, ready for the next auxiliary onslaught. Fingers crossed!

Surprisingly, we slept well. It must have had something to do with the soft, womb-like drone of the boat's engine. I was woken by someone walking past (probably on the way to the toilet) and noticed the sky beginning to slowly light up. I was on the opposite side to where the sun had set the previous night. You can't really do the sunrise or the sunset total justice when taking a photo, but I took out my little semi-automatic Ricoh camera and attempted to capture the scene.

I must admit I loved sitting and watching everyone waking up, listening to loud yawns and arms and legs stretching out. It was great watching the deck morph from a sea of colourful cocoons into human beings. Everyone looked worse for wear and we probably looked the same. There was no lippy or any of those so-called beauty products. The only skin cream worth having would be sun cream. Some people had deodorant, which was fair enough given that it was a very warm and humid environment. There was also a clammy consistency on our skin. The only thing I could put that down to was the sea salt in the air. I then thought about everyone on this particular deck. They all had a story to tell. It was something that I had often thought about and to be honest, I still do. Although I was aware of other people having different backgrounds, it was the first time that I had applied it to a group of people en masse. Maybe it was because I was away from all the pressures and monotony of routine and I had lots of time to recover from the things that chain us to our respective societies and lives. It was very much like a fog lifting and being able to see people and situations for what they were/are and having the ability and time to think clearly. It was definitely a light-bulb moment.

Our breakfast comprised of a couple of Israeli semi-hard croissants and water. While we were busy munching away, Lisa was talking about the moment she'd woken up during the night. She said that she'd thought she had died as the deck was very still and a thin layer of mist was hovering above everyone. Lisa mentioned that it was a very eerie and surreal moment and that it initially scared her shitless! It's totally understandable. I think I would feel exactly the same.

Now it was that time again. Yes, it was toilet time! There was still no change in the men's powder room. It was still stagnant, rancid and marinating well. Lisa reported the same. When you've got to go, you've got to go. The call of nature can be merciless, ruthless and vicious in a manner of speaking!

We packed everything up, which wasn't much, and hung around until we docked at Limassol. Passport control and security were a breeze compared to Israel. In other words, it was non-existent. Once in Cyprus, we headed straight for a sandwich bar and then grabbed a service taxi to Paphos. In case you don't know, a service taxi is basically a shorter version of a stretch limo, which is usually a Mercedes. They can carry seven people maximum and mainly travel between the major cities and towns across Cyprus. These types of taxis are also used in Israel. In Israel, they're called Sheruts. It's cheaper to use this service compared to the normal cab. Alternatively, there's always the bus, which is even cheaper.

We travelled along the coastal road, passing Aphrodite's Rock, also known in Greek as *Petra tou Romiou*, which translates into *Rock of the Roman*.

According to Greek mythology, this was the birthplace of the goddess Aphrodite. It was pointed out to us by the taxi driver, who by the way was the only one in the taxi who wasn't a nervous wreck. He was simulating emergency stops at every junction and bend on the road. This man, with one over-tanned arm, was a total fruitcake. He never stopped for anything! As he drove, his right arm hung out of the window... that explained his over-tanned arm. To add to our little episode, he pretty much chain-smoked the whole way. If crashing into an oncoming tractor wasn't enough, we had to contend with passive smoking and potential respiratory problems.

He dropped us off at the Paphos International Youth Hostel (IYH). It was nothing like the one in Tel Aviv. This looked like it was built from mud bricks and sandstone about three thousand years ago. I'm not exaggerating one bit! We climbed out of the cab, relieved to be on terra firma and glad to be alive. We checked to see if it was the IYH as it was literally the pits. To our horror it was! It had the IYH logo on the wall. It was worse and more expensive than the Gordon Hostel and that's saying something. Resigned to the fact that it was the hostel, we booked in and were given a room, bed, fleas and potential dysentery. The men and women were separated into different dormitories. This was going from bad to worse. There was no air conditioning, no fans and we hadn't even checked out the communal toilet and showers yet! But you could smell the not-so-sweet aroma of bleach hiding someone's recent dump. I'm not sure which aspect of that was worse... the dump or the bleach. There were definitely going to be a few cockroaches and mosquitoes hanging out come sunset. I suppose it was something to look forward to!

The hostel was situated in a quiet residential area and it was a good thirty-minute walk to the town centre and harbour. We walked it on the first day there but I couldn't see us walking that distance in the heat every day. So, the next day we hired out a couple of mopeds which were quite cheap. They were great fun and we could get around very easily and quickly. They were definitely worth the money.

My brother was due to be in Paphos with his family during that week, but was not arriving until the latter part of the week. Before I left the UK, he wrote down the address of where he would be staying and I said that we would try to turn up on a day that we had arranged. Until then, Lisa and I would potter and explore Paphos on the mopeds. One place that we visited was the Tomb of the Kings, which was interesting. It apparently dates back to around the third or fourth century BC. It's situated on the coast and was basically a burial site for the rich and powerful of the time. They were buried with their belongings, which included jewels and the like in some rather ornate, pillared underground tombs. Unfortunately, the tombs had been pillaged by grave robbers... similar to what happened to the Egyptian Pharaohs. I must admit, I did find the whole site intriguing. The fact that they called it a necropolis, which means *City of the Dead* which is a great Clash track, conjured up all sorts of images about black and white, tacky second-rate B-movies.

Behind all the excitement, there lurked a potentially large problem with me entering Cyprus. If I didn't have the relevant paperwork to leave Cyprus, it would mean that I would have to do National Service because my dad was a Greek Cypriot. So, I had to go on a two-hour journey to the capital, Nicosia, to get a replacement certificate that would get me off the island in one piece. I already had one but I was told by the officials at the Port of Limassol (and I say 'officials' loosely) that I would have to renew it.

Lisa pottered in Paphos while I practised my braking skills in the passenger seat of the service taxi which was taking me to the government buildings in Nicosia. As is typical of bureaucracy in all countries, I was shoved from pillar to post, told to go here, there and everywhere until I ended up in the right department, having taken two boxes of valium in the process. Fortunately, the lady on the other side of the window spoke good English, which was just as well because my Greek was not that great. I could just about keep up with a five-year-old and even then it would still be dodgy. She asked me if I had an existing certificate which I did. I tentatively took the document out and lovingly unfolded it, making sure that I didn't rip it. It was quite delicate. In other words, it was old and losing its structural integrity. That's a good *Star Trek* term! I was given the certificate at the age of seventeen by the Cypriot Consulate in London. It had definitely seen better days!

The first I'd heard about this certificate (which translated means *Licence to Leave*) was when I was over in Cyprus with my mum. I was about fifteen at the time. To be honest, I didn't really want to be in Cyprus with half of the North London Cypriot population. Anyway, we were at the airport about to leave Cyprus. We were going through passport control when an official pulled me to one side. He looked at my passport and asked me to sign a document so that I could leave the country, which I thought was strange. For some reason, and I can't remember why, I was ahead of my mum and she shouted out not to sign anything until she saw what it was. The document was all in Greek so I wouldn't have had a clue what I'd be signing. She rushed over and started reading the document. I'm so glad she did as it was a document saying that when I eventually reached the age of eighteen, I would have to do National Service for two years in Cyprus. I remember feeling shocked, really annoyed and disappointed with the Cypriot authorities. What a dirty trick! My mum was brilliant. She totally ripped them apart. She was good like that! She insisted that when we got back home, I should get one of these certificates for when we went back... not that I wanted to go back. When I told my mum that Cyprus didn't really do it for me, she said, "You're Greek, you go to Cyprus, no other place matters". That was the kind of mentality I had to put up with as I was growing up. This attitude wasn't just from my mum but my relatives and the Cypriots from school. I kicked back from the expected nationalistic view even from that age. I'm happy to say that I had other ideas. Every country and culture encourages this self-righteous view. I don't really agree with things like that. Having said that, it's OK to be proud of your country and culture, but I draw the line when problems and self-serving issues arise from it. Anyhow, in time, my mum eventually understood what I was saying and I respected her for it. She saw the sense in what I was saying and would often agree with me – not always though.

Anyway, I'm deviating again. Back to the lady behind the counter in Nicosia dishing out the *Licence to Leave* certificate. The certificate was in Greek and I didn't really have a clue what it said. It could have been a bus ticket for all I knew. The lady looked at my crumpled parchment, which at first glance could have been mistaken for a treasure map, and said, "This particular certificate is valid and always will be…you don't need another one". I was initially over the moon. I then became increasingly annoyed with myself for not getting someone to read and translate it to me word for word. What's more, the port official even saw it and it was even his suggestion to go and get it renewed. It begs the question, could he actually read? It didn't need renewing! What a complete waste of time! So, back to Paphos I went by service taxi, where I could continue to assess and improve my braking and wincing skills, while chewing my fingers off.

Historically, you have to bear in mind that these were the times when mobile phones were in their infancy. They were just beginning to enter our lives, so the huge majority of people didn't have them and that included us. In those days the phones were expensive and were the size of a house. Well not quite that big, but you get the picture! It's not something I really wanted as I liked the idea of not being contacted; going off-grid, so to speak. Lisa and

I had arranged to meet at a rocky area on the seafront near a certain café at some point in the afternoon. Who needs a mobile phone to arrange a time and meeting place? When I eventually arrived, Lisa was talking to a young guy. I went over to them to say hello and Lisa introduced me to him.

"This is my friend Nicc. I told you about him."

I immediately picked up an unwelcome vibe from him. I was not really surprised by that. I'd probably appeared at the wrong time just as he was about to deliver his final enticing line regarding his etchings! He apparently came over to Cyprus from Beirut in The Lebanon, on his dad's helicopter and was living in his family's apartment somewhere in Paphos. Clearly, someone had quite a bit of cash to splash and it wasn't us! I got the impression that he usually got what he wanted.

He invited us both to a club that evening and to be honest, I was absolutely knackered and I wasn't very keen. After all, it had been a long day and by the sounds of it, was about to get even longer. Somewhere in our conversation he asked me if Lisa and I were together. I said that we were friends, and again he looked at me suspiciously. Did he want me to say that we were an item? There's really no pleasing some people! Maybe I should have said that we were a couple just to shut him up! I don't really know why we didn't in the first place...

We went back to the sandstone insect hostel and I told Lisa about what had happened in Nicosia, freshened up a bit and we had a bite to eat in the Old Town. After torturously searching, we found the club in some old backstreet and he was waiting outside with two rather big blond guys either side of him. Apparently, they were Swedish... not that it mattered either way. We weren't introduced but I named them Bjorn and Benny, but they were beyond doubt no Dancing Queens. The rich dude looked a little odd to say the least. He looked bit like Danny DeVito with a quiff, being sandwiched in between Arnold Schwarzenegger and his blond double! It was almost comical without even trying to be. He then asked me the same question when Lisa was out of earshot about us being an item. He got the same answer, only this time I was being menacingly eyed up by what I can only describe as his henchmen. I couldn't understand why he kept asking me the same question. How many times did he want the same answer? Did he want it in writing? Can't a man and women be just good friends with no benefits?

At this point, I was beginning to get a bit concerned about my own safety. We were in the club when a lot of this was happening. In and among the flashing lights and loud music, I found Lisa to tell her that I was feeling threatened by this guy and his two mates. I wanted to leave as I had grown very fond of my arms and legs. I had built up a very good relationship with them over the years, especially my legs! In the past they had got me out of so many questionable situations. We'd grown up together and had become quite close, as you would naturally imagine. We totally understood each other. They would run even before the thought entered my head. Now that's real understanding! However, there was a tiny problem about to be unleashed. Lisa wanted to stay. I obviously didn't want to end up in a Cypriot A & E department, having various parts of my body sewed back on, while using a whole bottle of Johnny Walker as anaesthetic. She was saying that they were OK and I kept saying that I feared for my bodily parts. In the end I decided to leave, while all the time trying to convince Lisa to come with me. I felt responsible and feared for her safety and naturally my own. After all, we didn't know them from Larry. Having said that, I knew Lisa was very capable and able to look after herself. So, I left her at the club and went back to the hostel, while all the time feeling worried for her. I hardly slept until I knew she back at the hostel. She eventually rolled up in the early hours of the morning. Looking back, it reminded me of the times when my brother would go out in the evenings and I would stay awake until I heard the garage door open and the key in the front door. Only then would I nod off. I remember the car distinctly. It was a white and green Ford Anglia Super. Google it. It's a great looking car. I even remember the registration number, which was KPU143C.

The next day the atmosphere between us was a tad frosty. By late morning everything was sorted out and was back to normal. She said it was fine and there wasn't a problem, which was good. Apparently, he was going back to Beirut the next day, which was a relief. It had been reported on a national Lebanese news network, that a local Beirut butcher was concerned and visibly distraught, as one of his prize metre-long meat cleavers had gone missing. It was last seen being loaded onto a helicopter bound for Paphos that morning!

That afternoon, we pottered around the harbour area and we had a look around the old castle, which is found at the end of the harbour. Apparently, it was originally built during the Byzantine period as a defensive structure to protect the harbour. We also hooked up with George the Pelican, who was the resident celebrity in those parts. Over the years he has had a few stunt doubles. We did a bit of shopping in the Old Town, which was quaint, and Lisa bought a dried-out gourd. It had been decorated and varnished with the seeds left inside and it looked like an obese musical shaker. It would certainly be interesting presenting it at Israeli security. Not only would they have to deal with her passport, but they would also have to deal with this gourd. They've been known to blow up suspicious bags and objects and this innocent-looking gourd would definitely fall into that category. Amazingly, Lisa still has it tucked away somewhere at home. Personally, I'd use it to improve my archery skills!

The next day we went to see my brother and his family. We basically sat, ate and chatted the whole afternoon. It made a change not having to fend for ourselves and being pampered, although it wasn't really pampering, but you get the gist. He took some photos of me to show our mum that I was still alive, just to put her mind at rest. I have to admit it was good seeing them and having a familiar chat. I told my brother about the exit certificate episode and that he had better get one. He said that he had already arranged to go to Nicosia to get it sorted out as he had never had one in the first place. He was as organised as ever!

Having said our goodbyes and all that, we left Paphos the next day. We went back to Limassol, where we spent time on the coast just killing time, waiting to board the ferry back to Haifa. In terms of food, we again bought some provisions for the ferry. This time we didn't have falafels. I was still eating meat then, so we bought a couple of large kebabs. They were big enough to devour half in the evening and the other half for breakfast, and cost us less than a pound.

It really amazed me how lax security was in Cyprus. Once through passport control, we were literally waved through without a second glance. Again, we were pretty much one of the first ones to board the ferry. The deck was already inhabited with bodies and rucksacks from Athens and Rhodes. We claimed our spot for the night on our luxury deck-class floor. The ferry left the port early evening with again, relatively clean toilets and we arrived back in Haifa twelve hours later. We once again had the pleasure of puddles of ammonia and whatever else was lurking in the cubicles. The contents of the toilet floors were lovingly transferred via well-worn footwear onto the deck floor that we had all been calling home for the last twelve hours. What a beautifully descriptive thought!

BACK TO ISRAEL

We again experienced the usual questions but this time they questioned us about what we had done in Cyprus. Lisa's passport was once again at the centre of their attention and they took her aside and questioned her. She explained what kind of passport it was (as if they didn't know) and that security at Tel Aviv airport had been fine with it. If they weren't happy with it, they certainly wouldn't have let her in when she had initially arrived nearly two weeks earlier. As for the gourd, Israeli security were predictably suspicious and were shaking and tapping it. Eventually, it was put through an X-ray machine. After it was given the all-clear, we caught a bus back to Tel Aviv. I had previously booked a couple of nights in the Gordon Hostel (hey, it was cheap) just for myself and I was mulling over what I was going to do once Lisa left. The beauty of travelling like this was that I could go anywhere I chose to, without answering to or checking with anyone. I was still in awe of the freedom of it all.

Lisa's flight back to the UK was a late night one, so she snoozed in the hostel for an hour or so and I sat and read. Afterwards, we wandered around aimlessly and eventually caught the bus to the airport. I asked Lisa to go and see my mum to tell her that I was *Alive and Kicking* (a great Simple Minds track) as I knew that she would be worried. It's very understandable. Lisa checked in, we said our goodbyes and I saw her disappear through passport control, wondering whether the gourd would be the centre of attention again. Apparently, Israeli security questioned Lisa about her passport, where she'd stayed in Israel, why she went to Cyprus, who she went with, etc. They emptied her rucksack in full view of all the passengers and rifled through everything, including her smelly smalls. They ran a metal detector over her, which bleeped. They ran it over her twice, by which time they ushered her through to a private room where they searched her. Eventually, they realised that the metal they were picking up were the eyes of a tiger on the t-shirt she was wearing. All in all, you could say that it all went smoothly! But that really wasn't the case! Even our friend the gourd, also known as Gordon, was put through the proverbial mill. They were suspicious about Gordon and he was X-rayed again. I'm glad to report that he survived the ordeal and was able to tell the tale in his own sweet way, with some help from Lisa!

So, with Lisa safely deposited in the airport awaiting her flight, I made my way to the bus stop and waited to be transported back to my haven for the night. While I was sitting at the bus stop, a fellow traveller came and sat on the other end. It was a petite young woman with long, wavy orange hair which looked as if it was dyed with henna. It had that kind of look to it. Are you going to ask me how I knew it was henna? Are you asking me? Really? Well, I'm not going to tell you! OK! OK! I'll tell you! Just don't hassle me. The truth is, I've used henna a few times myself and I know what the finished article looks like. So, there you have it, I've used henna! What a revelation! It's not exactly a life changing piece of information, is it?

Let's put this amazing henna revelation to one side and I'll carry on with what happened next. I opened the conversation with a totally ground-breaking original line.

"I see you've just flown in!"

Her reply was, "Is it that obvious? I thought no one was going to notice!"

My bus-stop companion said this with an American type of twang and a big smile on her face. My immediate thought was that she had a good sense of humour and I do like a good sense of humour to feed off! In spite of this, I was picking up a standoffish vibe from her which was totally understandable. She actually seemed quite irritated and I put it down to either being tired from the flight or that it was me! In fact, it was neither. It was the hassle she'd got from Israeli security.

I was assuming she had come from the States. With that said I found out that she wasn't from America... she was Canadian. To be exact, she was from Montreal in the province of Quebec. Some people refer to it as French Quebec. It is situated on the east side of Canada with its official language being French. English speakers are a minority. There are groups in Quebec seeking independence from Canada – a bit like the Catalans in Spain. I must admit I made the mistake of asking her which American rock she'd crawled out from. While I was picking up my teeth from the bus-stop floor, she informed me that she was from Canada. Well, she actually said, "Canadaland" and then went on to say, while keeping a very straight face, that all countries should have the word 'land' at the end of them. So we went through different countries that could be renamed, such as Germanland, Italyland, Indialand and the list went on and on... most amusing! That's how I met Susy. She described herself as, "The crazy French-Canadian-Ukrainian Chick." Before you give me a hard time, they were her words, not mine and she certainly ticked all the boxes in the category of 'completely nuts'. We ended talking about Israeli security and how thorough and a pain in the arse they were. Evidently, she must be one of those who fit the dodgy profile. They pulled her bag to pieces, X-rayed everything she had, including her photographic gear. They took her Walkman apart and examined the inside saying that there was something unusual looking-inside. After giving her the third degree with the standard questions, she was greeted with "Welcome to Israel – you're free to go! Oh and by the way, hurry up and re-pack your bag!" This particular night shift obviously had a sense of humour. I curiously asked her about her Walkman.

"Did you put it back together?"

"Nah!" was her reply. "Do I look like a techo geek type? Those fascists screwed it back together and it had better work or else!"

As the bus approached, I said to her that I didn't think she'd get much joy with the 'or else' bit. She agreed.

Once on the bus we chatted until we arrived in Tel Aviv. Susy had booked herself into a decent hotel for a couple of nights. She said it was something she normally did after a long flight and then she would slum it after. I suggested that we could maybe meet up in the afternoon and to my amazement she agreed. Result!

We met the following afternoon. Susy asked me where I was staying, so I took her to see it. The reaction was great. She said that she had stayed in worse places. We eventually ended up going to Dizengoff for a falafel and just hung out together. The next day we walked around and generally chatted and had a laugh. She was good to be around… very funny! During the day, she had to go to a kibbutz office to confirm a kibbutz booking she had previously made in Canada, so I tagged along like one would. When we were at the office, Susy asked me if I had any plans to spend any time on a kibbutz. She asked me if I wanted to join her on the kibbutz, which came as a bit of a surprise. I'd only known her for a day and a half. I decided to say no as I just wanted to travel. To stay on a kibbutz would tie me down and it was something that didn't appeal to me. In saying that, we would be travelling and spending time together for the next few days, which was fine by me. I had nothing else to do.

The following morning, we left Tel Aviv for Jerusalem. It was beginning to feel a bit like *Groundhog Day* (the film). After surviving a bus station bomb evacuation due to a bag that was left unattended, we boarded the bus. We were nearing the outskirts of Jerusalem, when Susy dropped a bit of an interesting bombshell. She said that she'd 'forgotten' to mention that she was carrying a letter from her friend in Montreal. She had to give it to her friend's boyfriend in Jerusalem, who was expecting the letter. Big deal, I hear you say! Well, it was a bit of a big deal as her friend was Jewish and her friend's boyfriend, whom Susy had met once before, was Palestinian. It was a good job Israeli security didn't find it, otherwise who knows what would have happened.

Susy had to find him and give him the letter. She had been given his phone number and was to ring him for the address. She managed to contact him and wrote down his address. She also asked him if it was ok for me to come along. Susy mentioned to me in passing that he had reluctantly agreed. I wasn't too happy about it but I went along with it anyway. Why did I go along with it? I don't know, is the simple answer. The whole thing about the letter and ringing him for his address was not sitting well with me. Surely Susy's friend would have his address? Instead of her friend putting Susy through all this, why couldn't she just post it? Wouldn't you question it? Anyway, regardless of any possible consequences, I rightly or wrongly carried on.

His address was within the Old City walls in the Muslim Quarter, which was more or less just inside Damascus Gate. It's a lovely looking gate. From the road, there are a series of stone steps leading down to the gate itself. High above the gate, on the ramparts, stood a couple of Israeli soldiers observing the crowd. Was that meant to instil any confidence in my present predicament of my own making? Nope, not at all, would be my response!

After searching high and low and asking around for this particular address, we eventually found it. For some reason I thought that it would be a house. Don't ask me why I thought that; I just did. However, finding it was a bit of a relief tainted with apprehension. Our rucksacks were getting a bit heavy and we were getting a bit whiffy and soggy in the armpit regions. I'm not even going to mention the other regions. I wouldn't want to be a postman in the Old City. It must be a complete nightmare. Anyway, having finally found the address, which incidentally wasn't a house, Susy knocked on the steel door of what seemed like a flat. I would imagine having a steel door would definitely keep unwanted guests out and keep others in!

Like I said earlier, I didn't have a good feeling about this, but I was still going along with it, like a mouse about to nibble on a sweaty piece of cheese in a mousetrap. Could this guy behind the steel door possibly be the same guy from the café, wielding his knife and promoting his mother's baklava? The chances of that happening would not be very probable but not impossible. I had a scene in my mind unfolding about his mum beckoning me over to a tray of freshly baked baklava and then being fed by her delightful son, using his own delicate technique. That would be something to look forward to, don't you think? I told Susy about that night and she answered by saying, "If you were an Ancient Greek Hoplite you could have head-butted him with your helmet and tickled him to death with the feathers adorning the top of it". I started guffawing as I found it ambiguously funny. I had to explain to her why I was laughing so much as she thought it was funny but not that funny.

Like I said, Susy knocked on the door. The door opened slightly and this guy's head appeared. He had short, dark hair and was clean shaven. I almost wanted him to ask us what the password was, just like they did in the movies. The whole thing felt like we were trying to gain entry into an illegal poker den full of wrinkled old men smoking cigars bigger than their noses. Meanwhile, there'd be half-drunk bottles of whisky on the table with someone holding a sawn-off shotgun, ready to separate someone from their genitalia.

He quickly scanned Susy up and down smiled, and said, "Hello". He did the same with me apart from the smile and stared at me for what seemed like an eternity and then smiled. He then fully opened the door as if to say, come into my lair.

To my surprise his place was lovely. It was very authentic and very clean. On the far wall opposite the door, you could see the original huge blocks of stone and arches that met the well-worn stone floor. The floor itself was covered by small decorated rugs every so often. It seemed very homely and the guy was very friendly. He warmly welcomed us in. Was it an act? Who knows but he seemed fine... for now.

Once inside I found it quite cool. It was nothing like the humidity outside. I would imagine it be cold during the winter months, especially as Jerusalem is on a hill. He insisted we take off our rucksacks and sit on a tiny sofa he had. As we were sitting making small talk, I noticed a door leading to what I assumed was his bedroom. There was a small stone corridor which I found out later, housed the toilet/shower on one side and the kitchen area on the other. I didn't know what to expect but as I mentioned earlier, it was pleasantly clean and well-ordered.

He was very hospitable and asked us whether we had eaten and did we want a drink? We said no to the food because we didn't want to put him out. We said that we'd grab something later. However, we both had a fresh mint tea, which was luscious. It always tastes better when someone else makes it for you, don't you think? I was bursting by this point, so I went to the loo fully knowing that Susy would give him the letter. I made myself scarce.

Earlier, I asked Susy if she knew what was in the letter and whether she was nosy enough to steam it open. Personally, I was dead curious to know its contents. She said she was interested just in case Israeli security found it. She didn't want to be put in a compromising situation while knowing what was in it. I thought that it was an odd answer as Israeli security would have ripped her apart either way. Her friend reassured her that it was just a soppy letter and that THERE WAS NOTHING TO WORRY ABOUT! Well, those six words are a bit like the kiss of death. It's similar to a football club saying that they are happy with their manager and then sacking him the next day. Anyway, as it turned out, Susy didn't have the foggiest what was in the letter. That was the present situation. So, I nervously thought that we'd see how things unfolded.

The guy invited us to stay a few nights, which was great. He'd only met Susy once. I didn't know him from Larry and it was likewise for him. Given what was going on and what could potentially happen, I was starting to weirdly relax a bit but I did have that niggly sense of uneasiness. It was definitely a risky business. It might have been all legitimate and honest but I just didn't know. The worrying thing from my point of view was that I didn't get the hell out of there. I can't even answer to this day why I stayed and played along with the whole scenario. Maybe, I was giving him the benefit of the doubt. Maybe, deep down, I was kind of stupidly enjoying the whole thing. It was a bizarre situation.

Susy and I decided to go out for a few of hours, which he was fine about. Just before we left, he asked us if we wanted to go to Hebron with him when we got back. We agreed to go. We left our rucksacks leaning up against the wall, thanked him and left. Susy and I discussed the possibility of him going through our bags. We both agreed that it was likely, but the only things he would find were smelly clothes and other nasty garments! With that discussed, we headed off into the Old City looking for food... falafels again. Naturally!

Now, Susy was a keen photographer and she took pictures of most things within reason. She was in the process of setting up her own photography company and wanted various pictures as part of her gallery. Digital cameras were not around at the time, so it was film that had to be developed when she got back home. She also had to be mindful of how many photos she was taking. In Susy's case she was lucky as she had her own darkroom... lucky girl! In saying that, she would probably spend a long time developing the photos. Otherwise, she would have had to pay a small fortune to have them developed. Regarding digital cameras, it's all a lot easier now. All you need is an SD card and you can keep or delete pictures as you go along. It's a no-brainer really!

We headed back to Susy's friend's boyfriend's place (I hope that makes sense) to meet him to go to Hebron. He said he had something to take care of. Was it me? Was it us? Were we the part of "something to take care of?" Yes, I was suspicious, that he was suspicious, that I was suspicious of him. I really hope you can decipher that one!

Once we got back, all three of us walked out of the hustle and bustle of Damascus Gate and into his car. It was parked in a side road pretty much opposite Damascus Gate. The car was an old, red and dusty Renault 4 with a fair amount of rust. The paintwork blended in well with the rust. I couldn't see where the paintwork finished and the rust started. I wouldn't be at all surprised if it was held together with chewing gum, courtesy of Bazooka Joe. If you don't know who Bazooka Joe was, look him up.

I noticed his car had white number plates as opposed to yellow number plates. I'd seen both types of number plates around but I hadn't asked why there were two types. I kind of knew the reason for having different coloured number plates but I asked him anyway. The answer was simple. It was so that the Israeli authorities can identify Palestinian and Israeli cars at a glance. It was for security purposes.

Hebron is located south of Jerusalem on the West Bank and it took us about half an hour to get there. It's regarded as one of the four holy sites by some Muslims and is ranked the second holiest city after Jerusalem by Jews. The population is unhealthily split. There are estimated to be around 200,000 Palestinians compared to around 1000 Jews, who live on the outskirts of the Old City. Historically, Hebron has had its fair share of comings and goings and if you have any time, it's definitely worth reading about it. Hebron is often described as a microcosm of the Israeli-Palestinian conflict. Apart from this very brief excursion into Hebron, in hindsight, I now wished I had taken the time to spend a few days in Hebron. At the time, I had no idea of its political and religious significance. Like I have said, do have a read, it's really interesting. You can find information about Hebron online or better still, in a book. I absolutely love books!

So, there we were, chugging along in this little old Renault 4, which incidentally had its gear lever hanging out of the dashboard. I once had a battered old Renault 5 with exactly the same thing. Great fun to drive and it cost me the paltry sum of £90. I literally bought it purely on the gear lever novelty. I named my little, grey and priceless piece of metal Francoise!

Moving swiftly on from Renaults, I was looking out of the window and I have to admit that I was getting somewhat nervous. I was assuming Susy was feeling just as uneasy. She kept asking him questions with no straight answers. The sun was beginning to set as we came into Hebron. My first impression was that it was looking a bit sorry for itself but I suppose we were on the outskirts. We didn't actually go into the centre of the city but I would assume there would be shops and stalls selling virtually anything and everything.

As we drove, you could smell the food being lightly cremated as the aromas made their way into the evening air and into the car. I was beginning to quite like what I saw and my mind began to drift into thinking that this wasn't so bad. The next thing I knew was that we had stopped at some traffic lights. Susy suddenly yelled out something about a camel. I leant forward and saw that she had covered her eyes. I asked her what the hell she was talking about. I'm sure our host knew why. He turned around and looked at me, as I was in the back seat and laughed. He obviously found it funny. He pointed to half a camel hovering in mid-air. It was a butcher's shop. The camel was cut symmetrically from its head to its tail and it was then that I realised what Susy was screaming about. It's not every day you see the insides of a camel staring at you from across the road.

Its one thing seeing well-packaged pieces of meat in supermarkets but witnessing a dead animal hanging in full from a rail is something else. I wonder what people would do if they saw the animal being led to the slaughter, hung up to dry and then packaged. Would they think differently? I was beginning to head down the route of vegetarianism but I hadn't quite committed to it at that time. It was something I definitely wanted to do and I eventually did stop eating meat. It wasn't from the point of view of being healthy. It was more from the point of view that we do not have the right to kill or disrespect any animal or insect in any way. The lyrics to The Smiths song *Meat is Murder* stand out for me, especially the final line: 'Oh... and who hears when animals cry?'

With that said, my mind then started to paint ridiculous pictures of Susy and I hanging from meat cleavers in a backstreet establishment, with our host looking lovingly on. Sometimes the mind is such a great comfort, don't you think? We carried on driving a little further when we pulled up on the side of the road. The guy told us to stay in the car while he got out and ran across the road. He was gone around ten minutes, when he jumped back into the car with a face that looked as if he had been slapped with a wet fish and said, "It's done!" I was thinking along the lines of, "What's done? Are we to end up like the camel?" With that thought firmly embedded in my mind, we drove back pretty much in silence. I didn't say much, Susy didn't say much and our host definitely didn't say much.

Something had definitely concerned him when he had had his meeting. I could have put it down to tiredness as it had been a long day but then again, was I being too kind? Who knows? I wouldn't say that he was in a joyous mood as we drove back. Something had upset him. I knew that much for sure but it wouldn't be me asking him if he was alright. Judging by the lack of conversation from Susy, she was not going to ask him either. She was obviously picking up the vibes as well. It was definitely an odd evening. After what felt like forever, we eventually got back to the flat, where we all decided to turn in for the night. With all this going on, he was still very hospitable and charming and he continued to be the perfect host.

The following morning, I was woken by someone tentatively walking around. Initially, I thought it was Susy possibly going to the toilet. Then almost immediately, I heard the front door open and close. Had someone walked out? Had someone been let in? I looked up and checked the time. It was six thirty give or take a couple of minutes. My faithful old Timex watch would often lose a minute or two. As far as I knew, there was no one in this homestead other than me and Susy. She was still in her sleeping bag, making some weird and wonderful noises. I invariably brought up these noises in many conversations, which often resulted in me being punched, slapped and pushed. So, it obviously had to be our host going out. Off to work? Maybe! Well, he didn't mention he was going off to work last night. Had he run out of milk and bread etc? Possibly.

With those thoughts in my head and drifting back to sleep on the hard stone floor, I was suddenly awoken again by the door opening and closing and I saw our host standing over us. I checked the time again and it was about an hour later. He started saying that we had to leave immediately. I came round pretty quickly. There was an urgent tone to his voice that made me feel very uneasy. I had already been on edge ever since I'd first found out about the letter that Susy was going to deliver to him. Susy started stirring when the door was slammed shut. She rubbed her eyes and asked what the hell was going on. He stood over us and repeated that we had to leave straight away; to take our bags and go. I told Susy that we had to leave. He gave no explanation apart from that it was too dangerous for him and for us. The atmosphere wasn't good. He seemed stressed, so we did what we were told. Naturally, we asked what was going on. He shouted back. "GO! GO NOW!" So as a matter of course, we legged it as best we could, not before gathering everything at breakneck speed.

Once we'd escaped with our lives, because that's how it felt, we headed towards Damascus Gate, constantly scanning around to see if someone was following us. We couldn't see anyone singling us out, so to speak, so we sat rather stupidly on a wall opposite the gate and wondered what on earth had just happened and why. I told Susy about what had materialised that morning. She said it could be that he'd changed his mind about having us to stay or something else was occurring. We discussed how his mood had changed when he returned back to the car in Hebron. Susy added that he was expecting her but not me, which was true. She then promptly punched me on the leg and said it was my fault with an amusing smile. Jokes aside, could I have been the problem here? I probably was! It wouldn't surprise me one bit.

I'm just going to fast-forward a few months from this point, so that you can get an overall picture of what was possibly going on in his head. Susy and I kept in touch and often wrote to each other across the 'pond', otherwise known as the Atlantic Ocean. She said that when she got back to Montreal, her friend explained what happened. It transpires that he and some others thought I was a possible secret service plant, a Mossad operative. To those that know me, can you imagine me in that role? Moi? A Mossad agent? It would be like Johnny English wreaking havoc across the Middle East. It didn't bear thinking about. I couldn't help laughing out loudly when I read it! I laughed so loud that my mum ran upstairs to my bedroom, breaking the land speed and stairs record all in one go. She burst through the door, armed with a nail-infested rolling pin and my polished Gat Gun. She had this weird revolutionary glint in her eyes as if to say, "Come on! Make my day, punk!" – she always did like a good action film. She was ready for whatever was to come next. That bit obviously didn't happen. After I had read the letter, I went downstairs to make a cuppa. My mother asked me what had made me laugh so loudly, so I told her.

She gave me one of those looks as if to say, "What the fuck have you been up to now?"

Anyway, our ex-host apparently went on to say that I was the reason for Susy being so brutally searched at Tel Aviv airport and that she had been tracked from Canada. Now, that was funny! I wrote back saying how the hell could I be blamed for her being so brutally searched? I had never met her before etc. I have to say that the whole conversation was all tongue in cheek. I added that we had met at the bus stop and that she came onto me first. Her reply was that I needed therapy! Susy had some brilliant one-liners. The only thing missing were the physical slaps and the punches with her replies. The small drawings of fists and open hands on her letters made up for them.

With that said, I wrote back saying that I really could have been a secret service plant at the bus stop and that she wouldn't have known. I found Susy's reply quite funny again. She wrote back saying that I couldn't be a secret service plant as I wasn't tall enough! However, I could get away with being a gnome with a fishing rod! This conversation spanned a good few letters. It was very funny! So, when all is said and done, it explained his mood when he got back into the car at Hebron. It also explained his panicky urgency that particular morning. Sadly, it all made sense now.

Now, let's get back to the steps at Damascus Gate. As we sat nattering, it started to dawn on us that we needed somewhere to stay. As it happened and very conveniently, just behind us was a run-down pile of bricks and plaster called the Faisal Hostel, which seemed like it could have been in competition with the Gordon Hostel. It was above a mini-mart and it was accessed via a side door which was being blocked by what could only be described as a bouncer. He wasn't dressed in what you would describe as the dress code for a bouncer though. He was sporting a pair of clean, white trainers (YUK!), an oversized pair of black joggers with stains all over them and a black t-shirt with similar-looking stains. Around his chin he wore an unkempt beard, which looked as if he still had half his breakfast lurking inside it. Thankfully nothing was moving. Yes, I did have a good look! We asked him if there were any available rooms, beds, sofas, floors or rooftops for us. Anything would do for now. He shouted something up the stairs in Arabic. At the top of the stairs, a shiny head popped around the corner and said, "Welcome to the Faisal hostel. Please come up the stairs".

Up the creaky, wooden stairs we climbed and we were greeted by the rest of his body. He introduced himself as Faisal who just happened to be the owner. Such an odd coincidence, don't you think? I have to say his English was pretty good. Apparently, the only beds available were a couple of squeaky, metal-framed ones in the mixed dormitory area, which led onto a balcony overlooking Damascus Gate. It was a great view but was it too close for comfort after this morning's drama? Yes, of course it was! We both said that it would probably be fine and we tried to reassure each other as best we could. To be honest, I don't think our minds were put at rest.

He showed us around and it was fine. He included free tea and coffee in the price and the toilets were clean, as were the showers. He went on to explain why he had to have 'security' at the door. He said that there were people wandering in and stealing possessions. Faisal advised us not to leave anything valuable in our rucksacks. As if we would! The only thing of value that I had were my traveller's checks, which were plastered all over my body with wallpaper paste. They were a bugger to get off! Body waxing had nothing on this! Anyway, that certainly filled us with confidence about the place as you would expect!

We decided to have our base camp at the Faisal hostel for the next few days, which was great fun. It was a good location and we spent a lot of our time sitting and drinking tea and coffee, while watching everyone go about their daily routine.

One afternoon, just below us, outside the shop, all hell broke loose. Two women were arguing over what seemed to be a bag of tomatoes. How did we know there were tomatoes in the bag? Well, we didn't know at the time but read on and you'll see how we found out. The two women were shouting at one another in Arabic. One of the women was trying to liberate a white plastic bag from the other lady, who was holding onto her prize possessions for dear life. As they were tussling, the bag split open and some tomatoes fell out and onto the ground. They were still intact. Once on the ground, the woman who was trying to snatch the bag started stamping on the tomatoes – an event we aptly named the 'Damascus Gate Tomato Dance'. To us it was a pretty obvious name for an amusing scene. That was our reference to the whole thing. While the dancing was reaching its climax, one of the women (the one who originally had the bag of tomatoes) pulled out a knife and started threatening the other lady. It didn't just stop there. It escalated to a point that we were unwittingly involved. It was my new friend from Canadaland that set the ball rolling once again! First, delivering a letter which she shouldn't have had and now this! Never a dull moment but looking back, it was a lot of fun.

Susy ran back into the room, excitedly grabbed her camera and started taking pictures from the balcony. At this point, two men who were walking by had become involved and were trying to calm the situation down. As Susy carried on clicking away, one of the ladies looked up and pointed at her. She said something to the other lady and the two men. Suddenly, they were all united against the common enemy – Susy and her camera! Forget what the original argument was about. Forget the knife. Forget the squashed tomatoes. To them, this was far more serious. Someone was taking pictures of it all! They were all shouting and waving their arms, at which point more people entered the gladiatorial arena. Looking down, a fair-sized lynch mob was starting to emerge

The two men, closely followed by the two women, were making their way towards the stairs to the entrance of the hostel. According to Susy, and she was deadly serious about this, I had to do something to protect her from whatever was going to happen. I was trying to say to her that it was going to be fine and that it was just a lot of hot air. So, I grabbed my book and started to look as if I was reading. I suggested she should to do the same. She replied by saying,

"What's bloody wrong with you bloody Brits? They're going to kill me and you're lying there reading a bloody book and telling me to do the same!"

While she was having a proper French-Canadian meltdown, the noise from downstairs was getting nearer and somewhat louder. We then saw Faisal run past our dormitory door towards the stairs. Then within seconds, he was slowly walking backwards, stopping outside our door with his hands stretched out in front of him. While I looked down at my book trying not to panic, Susy was in full-flow panic mode.

"We're going to die! We're going to die!" was her mantra, closely followed by, "And all you can do lay there and read!"

I kept trying to say to her that she should try and relax, show them that we weren't totally crapping ourselves (which we were) and act like dumb tourists, which on this occasion and many others, we had proven to be exactly that... dumb!

I have to say Faisal was great. He was the go-between, in that he was translating and trying to calm the situation. The women were waving their arms, shouting and pointing at Susy. Faisal explained to us that they wanted the camera and the film. He also went on to say that the ladies didn't like the fact that photographs were being taken of them. Susy turned to me and said that there was no way she was going to hand over the film or the camera. She was adamant. The fear seemed to have subsided and had been replaced with defiance. Faisal managed to calm everyone down. They eventually left but they were still being verbal.

Once the women were outside, we could hear them shouting again for a few minutes and then it all stopped. We didn't dare go out on the balcony to see what was happening. Faisal casually walked into the dormitory and started saying that we shouldn't have taken any photographs, which was a fair enough comment. He added that the ladies wanted the camera and they also wanted the film to be destroyed.

Faisal had apparently come to an arrangement with the ladies, saying that he would get the film from us and give it to them. However, they were not going to get the camera. The proviso was that they had to leave the hostel first. They grudgingly seemed to accept what Faisal had suggested. However, Susy was having none of it. She wasn't going to hand the film over. Faisal then asked Susy how many pictures were left to be taken on that particular film. Susy checked her camera and said that she had about six left. He then said that she should quickly take those remaining pictures and wind in the film and put it away. She would then put a new film canister into the camera and take a very quick handful of pictures. Once that was done, the three of us went downstairs, opened up the back of the camera and exposed the new film to the light in front of them. The film was then given to the ladies. Although Susy and I were initially sceptical (especially given the fact that one of the women had a knife) the plan worked like a dream. Susy got to keep her pictures, the ladies got a roll of exposed film, thinking that it was the same film and Faisal got some peace. He should've been a Member of Parliament.

Anyway, Faisal made us promise that we would not take any more pictures from the hostel. He said it was bad for his reputation and his rising blood pressure. I have to say that it didn't do our blood pressure much good either! Still, there was no harm done... thankfully! So now we were on double alert. I couldn't believe that we'd got into so much potential trouble in just a couple of days. It was crazy but believe it or not, it was fun! As for the security man on the door, where the hell was he in all this? Feeding the creatures in his beard? Probably!

That evening, after telling Susy about my earlier incursion into the Mea She'arim area with Lisa, we ended up heading that way. Yeah, I know. You don't have to tell me. I was a sucker for punishment. However, this time we were covered up and made sure we were not baring all and sundry to the Orthodox Jewish community. Susy wanted to go there to take some pictures but I made sure she knew what she was letting herself in for. If we were seen taking photos, we would pretty much be in the same situation as earlier that day. This time there would be no tomatoes involved. Instead, there would be the addition of a few hand-picked and crafted rocks heading our way. The difference here would be that we wouldn't have Faisal to rescue us. In all probability, we could potentially end up in a bloody big hole, with no saviour.

We eventually stumbled into the Mea She'arim area after munching on more stall-bought falafels in pitta bread and salad. Even though we were covered up, we still stood out like sore thumbs; there wasn't much we could do about that. We were still viewed with suspicion. Every time Susy took her camera out of her bag, I was looking around making sure we weren't seen. She stood behind telegraph poles and walls and I was foolishly standing in front of her like a human shield. While she was clicking away, I was busy thinking up excuses and the like, in case we were seen and confronted by someone brandishing a rock.

You'd think we would have learnt our lesson the first time around regarding taking photos (The Photos – another great band with Wendy Wu as the lead singer). The camera with its zoom lens was not a small affair either. It was quite bulky. Miraculously, we weren't noticed or stoned and Susy said that she had taken some great photos. I have to say, just like the first time when I was with Lisa, we had seen some amazing individuals and costumes.

Having successfully negotiated Mea She'arim, we headed back to the hostel and had coffees, cans of coke and some nibbles as we chatted away on the balcony with the occasional good-natured slap coming my way. Damascus Gate and the humid, moonlit streets were an idyllic backdrop. It was the most simple and perfect night. We just sat around laughing and talking as if we'd known each other for years, while listening to Susy's tape of The Cure; such a brilliant band. She had a tiny speaker connected to her Walkman.

Isn't it funny how you meet people and you hit it off pretty much straight away? I have always found that incredible, even to this very day. It's as if there is some kind of a spiritual link. I remember working in a school many years ago where I met a Teaching Assistant called Joan. It was pretty much the same thing. It was as if we'd known each other for years or if you believe in past lives, in a life before. There was a connection straight away. She was a good few years older than me and she immediately took me under her wing. Even to this day I refer to her as my adopted mother. Such a lovely lady!

Most mornings, Susy and I would walk a little way down the road to get our daily yoghurt and croissants. We had got to know the owner in the shop and he would often give us the off croissants. Being given stale croissants and pastries happened quite often as I travelled around. To be honest, they were fine. Along with the croissants, we had a small tub of yoghurt every morning which was good for lining our stomachs for the day ahead. That was our only routine for the day. One particular morning, after our luxury breakfast feast, while seated on someone's wall, we decided to go on an hour-long bus ride to Ein Gedi. It's actually a nature reserve and it's situated not too far from Masada and the Qumran Caves on the Dead Sea. I would say the whole area is pretty much dry but in saying that, it's absolutely beautiful. In fact, it's stunning.

Masada was an ancient fortress and the former palace of King Herod the Great, who was king of

Judea at the time. It was besieged by the Romans between 73 and 74 AD and it was famous for the final Jewish Revolt against Rome, where about nine hundred and sixty Sicarii rebels committed mass suicide, rather than be taken by the Romans. I did have a potter on Masada some time later which I'll tell you about another time.

The Qumran Caves are a series of caves, apparently where the Dead Sea Scrolls were found. The Dead Sea Scrolls are ancient manuscripts that consist of passages from the Old Testament and are said to be around two thousand years old.

The Dead Sea itself is just that... DEAD! It is totally absent of any life. There are no fish or plant life. It's a lifeless expanse of salt water. It's incredibly salty and the surrounding mud apparently has powerful healing properties, and can treat conditions ranging from skin conditions to back pain. The Dead Sea itself is geographically found between Israel and Jordan and is famous for being the lowest point on Earth at four hundred and twenty-three metres below sea level. It was very hot!

The journey to Ein Gedi was good apart from the descent. We were sat at the back of the bus and personally, it was really not the best place for me to sit. I was very nauseous as the bus made its way down to the Dead Sea. Susy was trying to encourage me, in her own sweet way, not to be sick. Her words of encouragement were a well-known slang dialect which included the phrase, 'dead meat'. I'll let you work out what she could have said. To be told not to be sick was easier said than done, especially when I had a potential liquid projectile lurking between my stomach, and the back of my throat. Anyway, in the end, the road levelled out and all was good.

Now, call me weird (say it louder because I can't hear you) but I love looking at rock formations and landscapes. I actually find all these formations spectacular. I must admit, I found the whole area around the Dead Sea fascinating. Susy had been to Israel and the Dead Sea before and she was saying that I would love it. She was not wrong. It was awesome! We got off at the Dead Sea Public Beach area which had showers, an expensive café and shop. Susy wanted to take some more photos of the area. While I stripped off and plastered myself with the Dead Sea mineral mud, she was busy snapping away at anything and everything for her gallery. This included people of all shapes and sizes smothering mud over themselves. I'm just glad that I wasn't wearing my well-worn, woollen budgie smugglers that my mum had knocked up on her Juki sewing machine! I know! The mind boggles!

I made my way into the sea with my new mud body mask. Susy apparently took a couple of sneaky pictures of me, which I found quite amusing. Once in the water I found it to be quite warm. I had a few cuts and grazes on my arms and legs, which almost immediately started to sting like hell. That was the salt doing its healing job. I wouldn't envy anyone who had haemorrhoids. I'd imagine it would be out-and-out agony. Once in, Susy was shouting orders in true military fashion from the shore. She said to lay flat on my front and back. She said that the huge amount of salt content in the water would keep me afloat. It was the strangest experience. It was literally impossible to sink. In fact, it took me a couple of minutes to get used to it. It was really bizarre. I tried to get Susy to come in but she told me to bugger off, using a few choice international phrases! She was too busy taking photos of people, the landscape and of my good self.

I washed the mud off in the sea with the sun belting down. It seemed to be getting hotter. I used the showers to wash the salt off as you could see it beginning to dry on my skin which made some interesting patterns. Susy began to take pictures of me showering and I'll add that as this point, I was definitely wearing my shorts. As she was clicking away and while I was calling her a Canadian perv, she said that showering scenes were good but she would probably put mine in a time capsule and have it buried very deeply! Once I was clothed, we grabbed a couple of the cheapest cold drinks from the café. As I mentioned earlier, the prices were extortionate. We wandered onto a rocky barren hill where there was no shade and yep, you guessed it, Susy took more photos in the midday sun! Mind you, I have to say the view was just stunning. As we sat on a rock with our legs dangling over the edge, looking over the Dead Sea, we could see further into Jordan. The whole area looked so perfect and serene. It was beautiful.

Once we were suitably frazzled, we decided to head back to Jerusalem and back to the hostel, as we were a bit wiped out. For the rest of the day, we just pottered around the Old City drinking and snacking. We bumped into Honey, the Jews for Jesus lady (remember her?) and we had a great chat about life and politics. It was an interesting couple of hours, especially as she was constantly buying us drinks and nibbles. We offered to pay our way but she insisted on paying, so who were we to refuse? She was a lovely person.

I know I've said it before and I'll carry on saying it, but this is why I wanted to get away from the UK and routine. I was able to do exactly what I wanted to do and this mind-set has stayed with me. So, for the next few days, we just wandered aimlessly, pottering around the Dome of the Rock, the Wailing Wall etc and generally amusing ourselves. However, we were also on high alert regarding the tomato dancers and Susy's friend's boyfriend. That's most unquestionably a bit of a mouthful!

Unfortunately, the day came to go our separate ways. I was a bit sad about it. Susy again invited me to join her to stay with her on her kibbutz. I must admit, the idea was more appealing to me this time as I'd got to know her. I was very tempted, but in the end, I decided to stick to my original plan and to just carry on enjoying this kind of nomadic existence. If I had gone, I could see myself becoming a bit too comfortable and predictable. It was something I didn't really want. We had decided to stay in touch so we exchanged addresses and that was that, apart from another bus terminal evacuation, due to a suspect package. What fun! Susy was heading north somewhere near Tiberias on the Sea of Galilee, where it is said that Jesus walked on water. I was heading south through the Negev Desert to Eilat on the Red Sea. We couldn't be further apart.

The Negev Desert covers around half of Israel's total land mass. You would think that a desert, any desert, would be totally destitute of life. However, the Negev is home to nomadic Bedouins, who have lived there for hundreds of years. Traditionally, Bedouins live in temporary accommodation (tents) and would move seasonally with their livestock. Along with the Bedouins, wildlife such as the Nubian ibex and the desert hyrax can be found there. In addition, there are some modern Israeli communities springing up and living alongside this environment.

Historically, the Negev boasts some amazing archaeological sites and rich cultural treasures. The largest city in the Negev is Be'er Sheva, which has a population of around 200,000 people. It's on the northern edge of the Negev. Biblically, Be'er Sheva is mentioned in Genesis. It is where Abraham, the founder of the Jewish people, made an agreement regarding land with the Philistine king, Abimelech of Gerar.

The journey from Jerusalem to Eilat by bus took around five hours, with a couple of short stops. It was quite a long trek but the scenery made up for it in no uncertain terms. It was spectacular. Going forward in time, one of the many places I ended up pottering around was the Sinai Desert (which was equally spectacular) Saint Catherine's Monastery and Mount Sinai. Again, that's another story.

Nature is such an awesome experience. I believe that we don't spend enough of our time experiencing the simple things in life. We become too embroiled in 'life'. We tend to spend too much time surviving and trying to dig ourselves out of social and material problems. These are situations we have either been fated to have, or that we have created ourselves.

Anyway, although the Egged bus was air conditioned, I still had to peel my sweaty t-shirt off the back of the seat. As I got off the bus, I was confronted by what seemed like a gush of heavy heat. I described the heat as 'heavy' because it felt as if I was jumped on by twenty-three belligerent Sumo wrestlers, all armed with hair dryers which had been set on the hottest setting.

After wandering around for a bit, I found a bed for a few nights. It was a place called the Happy Hostel, which had tea, coffee and... wait for it... jam sandwiches on tap. Having free tea and coffee is always enterprising enough but chucking in free jam sandwiches was just pure genius. It was a good job I wasn't diabetic, as I spent a lot of time making and nibbling these sandwiches.

The first people I met in the hostel were a group of four Scousers, who I must say were a total scream. They were so funny! They were good-natured guys but totally nuts and I do mean nuts! The banter was agonisingly hilarious. Three of them were Liverpool fans and one was an Evertonian. The odd one out got so much stick, I almost felt sorry for him! Nevertheless, it was all tongue in cheek and he gave it back very well. Of course, the fact that I was and still am a Liverpool fan was a definite bonus. This group were great fun.

They asked me why I supported Liverpool given the fact that I was from London and the answer they got back was this... I was looking for a team to support and I had narrowed it down to Huddersfield Town (why Huddersfield Town? I honestly couldn't tell you why) Chelsea (purely because of the shade of blue) and Tottenham (because they were local and that I thought Martin Chivers was a great footballer). It was 1971 and Liverpool and Arsenal were in the FA Cup Final. Liverpool had a very young team at the time with the likes Brian Hall, Alec Lindsey, Steve Heighway to name a few. Liverpool lost 2-1. The players were quite visibly upset and rightly so. It touched me so much that I started to support them. As a result my parents went on to buy me the LFC kit. Looking back, the funny thing about the whole kit thing was the shorts... they weren't red. They were a dark shade of pink. The sports shop called Briggs and Sons didn't have red shorts. Anyway, I have to add that at the time Liverpool hadn't really won much so for your information and a point of reference, I wasn't a glory hunter.

Geographically, Eilat is pretty much nestled between the Egyptian and Jordanian borders. It's situated at the most northern part of the Red Sea and at the most southern part of Israel. It is here that many people enjoy scuba diving and snorkelling activities. These activities didn't really appeal to me and in addition they were very expensive. That gave me the excuse to give them a wide berth. I spent the day wandering around the beach and coastal area, reading, listening to music and dodging low-flying, incoming and outgoing passenger jets. They were so low that if you looked hard enough, you could see the whites of the pilot's eyes and bits of latkes stuck in the crevices of their teeth. Apart from that, for me, there wasn't a great deal to do, so I spent the next few days pottering and hanging out with the Scousers. I consumed loads of tea and jam sandwiches at my leisure.

I eventually caught the bus back to Jerusalem. Mind you, I did toy with the idea of going into the Sinai Desert for forty years like the Israelites did. Forty years seemed a bit excessive so I decided against it. Unfortunately, I needed to get a visa from the Egyptian Consulate. To be honest, it was a lot of faffing around, so I decided to go another time, which I did (as I mentioned earlier). This was the beauty of what I was doing.

I arrived back in Jerusalem in the late afternoon and found a cheap hostel near the bus station and just basically slept. I also needed a little time to debrief myself. Just for you individuals with a wild imagination, debriefing in this case doesn't mean changing my underwear or any nether region activities. The sun and the journey had completely wiped me out. The next day, I was back on the bus making my way to Nazareth (nothing to do with the rock band). Thinking about it, though, Nazareth recorded a song called *Hair of the Dog* (have a listen... it's a great song) which is a colloquial term for a remedy for a hangover. In my case, this was an apt description of sorts but without the alcohol. My remedy for spending ten hours travelling to and from Eilat was to chill out for the night, have a good scrub and then get straight back onto the bus the next day. With that said, the amount of times I'd used them lately, I really should have bought shares in Israel's Egged Bus Company.

NAZARETH

On this occasion, the bus station had no suspect bags, so we left on time, not that there was any rush. During this journey of around an hour and a half, I was listening to Roxy Music and I came to the rapid conclusion that I wasn't really that keen on them. I'm not even sure why I took the tape with me. Maybe I could exchange it at some point. Anyway, I switched the tape to The Clash's second album, *Give 'Em Enough Rope*, which revived me as I was still a bit groggy from the past few days. I absolutely love everything about this album, from the cover design, to the production and of course, every song on the album.

Thinking back, it's a pity I didn't take any Nazareth tapes with me. Like I'd said earlier, such a great band! It would have been quite fitting listening to *Holy Roller* on the journey to Nazareth. The term 'Holy Roller', although a derogatory term, describes a member of a sect that expresses religious fervour in an ecstatic or frenzied way. I tend to relate these lyrics to some people I know, have known and to around half the population who live across the pond, not to mention other parts of the world.

Biblically, Nazareth was the place where Mary and Joseph lived. The Angel Gabriel appeared to Mary and said that she would fall pregnant via the Holy Spirit. While she was pregnant, they had to go to Bethlehem to register for the census, as Joseph, who was Mary's husband, originated from there. It's been estimated to be about a five-day journey by foot or by donkey. Nazareth was also the place where Jesus grew up and worked as a carpenter until he was about thirty. That was before he went to Jerusalem to give the Romans and the religious Jewish hierarchy a rather large headache. These days Nazareth is one of the biggest Arab cities in Israel with around seventy per cent of its population being Muslim, while the rest are Christian.

I got off the bus at the Central Station and started to look for a place to stay. I eventually came across The Sisters of Nazareth Convent. I didn't pay much attention to it until I saw a sign in English saying 'rooms for rent'. Well that certainly grabbed my attention, so I enquired and the only bed they had within my budget was in a same-sex dormitory. That was fine and I have to say that the communal toilets were spotless. I could eat a falafel off the floor... not that I would want to. The dormitory, as I expected, was rather sparse but very clean. It was probably the cleanest place I had stayed in so far. I didn't really expect much in the way of cleanliness regarding accommodation but for me, this was heaven... pardon the pun! Compared to the Gordon Hostel in Tel Aviv, this place was a 5-star rating! Although it was clean, it did have its fair share of microscopic residents. I have to say that I enjoyed staying there. It was buzzing in more ways than one but it felt safe and very peaceful.

Once I had settled in and had a read, I ventured out to have a look around, like you always do when you go to a new place. It's an unwritten rule! As it happened, not far from the Sisters' gaff was the Basilica of the Annunciation, which is part of the Catholic faith. This apparently was the site of the Angel Gabriel announcing to Mary that she would have a baby via the Holy Spirit, hence the name, Basilica of the Annunciation. That's makes sense, right? Well, I hope it does, as I'm not going into the whys and wherefores of the spelling of 'Annunciation' and 'announce'. The plain fact is that I haven't got a clue why the spellings are different. I'll leave it to you to investigate and get the instant gratification from the web.

It's a lovely building, both inside and outside. Once inside, I just wandered around until I came to what resembled an old doorway. It was apparently the Grotto of the Annunciation, which is believed to be Mary's childhood home and where the Angel Gabriel appeared to Mary. As a child, I'd heard about these events and stories in school and at home and to be honest, I really never paid too much attention to them. However, I was now able to piece these stories together by drawing up a mental map of what I had seen in Jerusalem and Nazareth. I actually found it to be quite interesting.

The Basilica was a good place to be. Not only was it quiet and away from the noise and chaos outside, but it was cool, which was a blessing in itself. After spending some time in the Basilica, I wandered over to the old market which like most markets, was a sight to behold... great colours and great smells. They were unquestionably messing with my senses. Mind you, I wasn't too impressed by the flies' air-bombing campaign targeting the meat.

The next day, after a good night's sleep and a hearty breakfast provided by some stoic nuns, I had it in my mind to visit some more churches in the area. While having our communal breakfast, I started talking with some other travellers and they told me about the other churches in the immediate area. I visited the Greek Orthodox Church of the Annunciation, which is located over an underground spring. It's claimed that this is where the Annunciation took place. According to Eastern Orthodox faith, Mary was drawing water from the spring when the Angel Gabriel announced the news to her. This was another interesting church. It was a lovely building with a beautifully decorated interior.

Next on the list was the church of St. Joseph. It's believed that this is where Joseph lived before he married Mary. Once married, this is where both Mary and Joseph lived. It is also believed that this was the site of Joseph's carpentry workshop and where Jesus grew up and worked.

The Coptic Church was the final church I visited. I found it to be quite interesting as the Coptic Church was founded in Egypt. By this point, I have to admit that I was all churched out! However, I found it hugely interesting that there were differing views and claims from the different Christian denominations – the Catholics claiming one thing and the Orthodox claiming something else! I suppose the same can be said about all the other faiths.

After milling around Nazareth for a few more days and having coffees and chats with some locals, not to mention a little job offer, I decided to buy a ferry ticket once again to Cyprus. This time I decided to visit a couple of relatives. One in particular was my

Uncle George. From there I could move onto the Greek island of Rhodes. I thought I would do the north of Israel another time. I needed a change for now.

As I mentioned earlier, I had a little job offer of three to four days' work in a small café. It's a place that I had hung out in and where I had hit it off quite well with the guys there. The person I was covering had to go somewhere. They didn't go into any detail as to why. It was none of my business. I don't actual mind the word 'business' in this context.

Well, in all honesty, I had nothing better to do and I could do with the money and free food. I started almost immediately, collecting plates and cleaning tables, etc. At one point they asked me to use a deep fat fryer to cook chips, which I didn't like doing. I actually ended up doing that pretty much all the time, when I wasn't *Cleaning Windows!* Sorry, George Formby got the better of me there. I meant to say when I wasn't cleaning tables. Easy mistake really! On the plus side, the fryer had a timer on it, which made lighter work of it. At times, I felt like I was feeding the five thousand but without the fish and the bread... just chips. It was too hot to be in the kitchen area all the time and I was given time to sit and chat in the cafe area when I wasn't chipping.

I have to admit that I was a little sad to leave Nazareth. I had made a handful of good friends in a relatively short time. Their names were Ibrahim, Hamza, Aziz and Habib. It was good to listen to their life stories, their families' life stories and what they themselves wanted from life. As they spoke, I remember comparing my younger days to theirs. It was a total contrast. Life is very much a lottery. We would often go out after the café had shut and we would sit around either eating or having a drink. There was so much laughter. They were so welcoming. I was even asked if I would like to have a meal around Hamza's parent's house. I obviously accepted.

When I turned up, I gave the family a small box of traditional sweets as a thank you. They were very grateful, just as I was grateful for having been asked to have dinner with them. It was the least I could do. These people didn't have much in the way of material things, but their hospitality was unconditional. There was no animosity or judging at all. It was a breath of fresh air. I had, and still have, total respect for these people.

When I informed Mustafa, the owner, that I was planning on leaving, he tried to convince me to stay a little longer. He went on to say that I had fitted in well and that he would be happy to have me as a son-in-law! He laughed and said that the only problem was that he didn't have any daughters. That was actually quite funny. I was very tempted to play on that and take it down another road, but I decided to keep my mouth firmly shut and laugh, as I do tend to say things that can go badly wrong. I'm very aware that I do have an odd and acquired sense of humour. With that said, he invited me to his modest home for a pre-planned family get together, along with the people I worked with. Once again, I felt very honoured, as I was with Hamza's invitation. Overall, I found Nazareth to be a very welcoming and a culturally diverse city but I had already bought the ferry ticket and I didn't want to waste it. In hindsight, having built up a nice little network of friends, I should have spent more time in Nazareth. It felt right.

Anyway, I said my goodbyes and caught the bus. I made my way to Haifa and spent the night in a lovely Christian-based hostel called the Bethel Hostel. I spent the evening talking about Christianity with the inmates and the owners. It was an interesting evening. It had a great atmosphere; everyone was so friendly. In the morning, after a good simple breakfast, I got talking to a couple of American guys who were also staying in the hostel. We teamed up for the day and wandered over to the Bahai Temple and its gardens, which were situated high on Mount Carmel, overlooking the city of Haifa and the port.

The Bahai faith is a relatively new religion. It was first developed in Persia in the 19th century. The faith teaches the essential worth of all religions and the unity of all people and rejects racism, sexism and nationalism... all the 'isms'. Apparently, the founder, Bahallah says:

"It is not for him to pride himself who loveth his own country, but rather for him who loveth the whole world. The earth is but one country and mankind its citizens".

Definitely sounds like a good one to me! You can imagine the persecution that the Bahai faithful must have suffered. If you get a chance to read about the Bahai faith, do so. It's fascinating. I have always said that it's one God / Universal Energy and one community. I have had quite a few discussions with people regarding this, often ending up agreeing to disagree. Forgive me for saying this, but to me, the Bahai faith is ethically similar to the *Federation* in *Star Trek*. Everyone seems is aware and respectful of all faiths and the traditions of the other species. They are pretty much united as one. There are a few exceptions, though. I often think that the writers were years ahead of their time.

CYPRUS (again)

It was mid-afternoon and time to go back to pick up my rucksack from the hostel. I made my way to the port where my evening's accommodation awaited. I felt that the officious Israeli security department were going to have a field day with me, as I'd been in and out of Israel a number of times in a short period of time. Armed with my customary falafel and croissants for the night's journey, I made it through customs totally unscathed, much to my disappointment. I wasn't free from the normal questioning and bag searches though; that goes without saying.

Once on board the ferry and yes it was the Vergina, I made my way to the rear part of the deck and claimed my spot for the evening. I watched as the floor space was gradually covered by rucksacks and sleeping bags once more. Again, I was on the perimeter of the deck and setting up camp next to a couple of Kiwi girls (New Zealanders to you) from Nelson, on the South Island. I made the mistake of assuming that they were from Australia, which didn't exactly go down too well... or so I thought. In fact, it was a huge wind up which I fell for, as did most of our fellow travellers in our immediate vicinity. After a couple of minutes of "How can you mistake us for Aussies?" they continued the relentless verbal barrage. After what seemed like an eternity, a cheeky grin appeared on one of their faces and the game was up. I was then given a quick phonics lesson in how you can tell the difference in the pronunciation of certain words, which was certainly helpful.

They were on their way to Athens, which would take them approximately two and a half days and would briefly stop in Cyprus and Rhodes. I told them that I was getting off in Cyprus to look up a couple of relatives in Larnaca. It was a money-saving exercise. Mind you, my relatives didn't know that I was about to stealthily descend on their doorstep. It should prove to be an entertaining excursion. The girls saw the logic in it, especially as budgeting was the order of the day. We chatted most of the evening, exchanging stories, including ones about the worst toilet facilities we had come across, and places we had been to and enjoyed while travelling. They were constantly taking the pee out of themselves which was funny. They were saying that humans were the minority in New Zealand and that sheep were the majority. They even said that some sheep had morphed into politicians and that they were running the country. Anyway, at that time, there were around sixty-five million sheep in contrast to an approximate human population of about three and a half million. Nowadays, the human population is around five million, while the number of sheep has dropped to around forty million due to the removal of government subsidies.

I find it quite interesting talking to people, listening to them talking about their lives and where they live. I would always unintentionally end up comparing their life experiences and quality of life to mine. It's not in a sense a bad thing and in no way critical. It's more an education in life... very much like I did in Nazareth. Staying on this subject, when I was in Tel Aviv, an English nineteen-year-old girl totally opened up to me while we were just talking. I suppose I've got one of those faces that you just want to punch or a vibe that says, "I can talk to this guy". I've been getting this all my life. I'm not complaining at all. I'm just happy that people feel comfortable to talk to me. Anyway, she was saying that she had been sexually abused by her father and had to get as far away as possible from the situation, just to feel safe and have some kind of peace. Apparently, no one from her family knew where she was, only that she was somewhere in the Middle East. I felt so helpless and so sorry for her. The only thing I could do was to listen to her and give her the space to talk. It just reinforced the fact that everyone has a story to tell, and everyone's story is a lesson for us all, in some way.

In the same vein, I know of two homeless people who I try to help as much as I can. They had fallen on hard times. The man used to work on the stock market and had made a huge mistake and ended up losing a horrendous amount of money for his clients. As a result, he had a breakdown over this, lost his job and eventually lost his flat. By the same token, his girlfriend had a breakdown, lost her job and her flat as she couldn't keep up with her rent. This seems to be quite a common pattern. They met in temporary accommodation, where she was abused by other temporary residents. They are both very intelligent people and steer away from drugs and alcohol.

I was recently reading that in Finland, the government have a policy to house the homeless. It's called the 'Housing First' concept. People who are affected by homelessness are given a small flat and counselling. There are apparently no preconditions. It's been reported that about four out of five people who are in this position make their way back into a stable life. I know that Finland's population is considerably smaller than the UK's, but surely the British government can help out in a similar way, for people to gain a foothold to recovery? So, as I said, everyone has a story to tell.

So we head back to life on the ocean waves. You can imagine Captain Pugwash with his hearty crew mates, including Master Bates and Seamen Staines, having a great time! I loved watching *Captain Pugwash* when I was a kid, but I was obviously not aware of some of the references until I was in my mid-teens. The writer's play on words was just brilliant.

So, as I was saying, it was turning out to be a good evening. Someone across the other side of the deck was playing a mixture of Bob Dylan, Leonard Cohen and Beatles songs on a black and white, 1967 Gibson Flying V guitar, backed up on a 1000-watt, thirty-foot tall, Marshall stack system. The singer was singing to the stars in the night sky and went by the name of Lemmy. If only that was remotely true! In our case, it was a battered, sunburst acoustic guitar with all sorts of stickers on it. Pretty soon most of us deck-class oiks were in full voice. It was a truly fantastic atmosphere. We were in the middle of the Mediterranean Sea, with not a soul around for miles, singing our little hearts out. We all eventually went to sleep on a high that evening. I might add that some were on more of a high than others.

I woke quite early that morning and watched the sun's rays break across our own personal moonlit horizon. It started out as a small arc of pure sunlight, reaching out to escape the dark ungodliness in which it was encased. I stood watching the sky and sea separate into their respective entities. Our planet is so beautiful, if only we would just sit and contemplate it. I don't think I've ever felt so at peace and content with myself. I was floating in middle of the sea with nothing but my thoughts. I find it difficult to put into words, but it was an amazing feeling. There was no pressure in any way, shape or form. I had very little money, no material goods; just *Me, Myself and I* (another great song by Joan Armatrading). I felt blessed to be able to experience this, if only for a short while.

Within a few hours of the sun exposing itself to us, we moored up at the Port of Limassol. I said my goodbyes to my Kiwi companions and treated myself to yet another whistle-stop tour of the Greek Cypriot port authorities. Once through, I jumped onto a cheap local bus which took the long, slow route to Larnaca. I was in no hurry to get anywhere, so this seemed perfect. We had a couple of toilet stops on the way and all in all, it was a not a bad journey. Apart from setting foot on Cypriot soil with Lisa, the last time I'd been to visit my relatives must have been about nine or ten years prior. I'd never been too interested in visiting Cyprus after the age of eleven, give or take a month, as I began to find it a bit of an ordeal. Most Cypriots go to Cyprus year in, year out without fail and personally, I couldn't do that. I still can't see the attraction. You fly two thousand miles and meet half of North London there, dripping in gold and Mercedes key rings. That's not for me, I'm afraid. In saying that, like a trooper and for the shoestring cause, I was willing to put up with it for a few days.

I finally decided to get off the bus at a point that looked familiar to me. It was the police station near the harbour. From memory, I kind of had a good idea where I was. Mind you, it was from a long time ago. In saying that, my sense of direction and memory was and still is pretty good, so I started walking. I was fully loaded and armed with my rucksack, orange-foamed Sony Walkman headphones strapped to my head and a smile, while listening to Bruce Springsteen's *Born To Run* album. In fact, I had four of Bruce's albums on two tapes and I seemed to be listening to them more and more.

I dodged most of the potholes, the partial and non-existent pavements and the crazy drivers on route to my destination. I eventually found the road in which my Uncle George lived. I recognised the local church at the bottom of his road so I started walking uphill towards his house. It was also where my grandparents used to live. My uncle lived in a rather large house made up of the main house, a large courtyard behind the house and three small buildings off the courtyard. They included a kitchen, an outside toilet/shower and another bedroom. Well, that's what I remembered from the last time I visited. I found the house and mustered the courage to knock on the door, which had not changed apart from the colour. As they didn't know I was coming, I was naturally a tad apprehensive.

So there I was on the doorstep. I took a deep breath and knocked with the large, metal ornate knocker. A rather large, grey-rooted, middle-aged woman opened the door after my second attempt of knocking. I immediately recognised my Aunt Dasoulla as she slowly opened the door. She hadn't changed much. It took a few seconds, but she recognised me, which was surprising given that fact that I was looking more than slightly on the rough side and that she had not seen or heard from me in years. It probably helped when I said who I was. She looked me up and down. You could almost hear her thoughts saying, "What the fuck do you look like and what do you want?" You know that look of disgust you get when people think you're a vagrant. On the other hand, maybe you don't. You may have experienced what my aunt was feeling, when you've seen someone in the street looking rather rough and made the effort to cross the road to avoid them.

If we weren't related, albeit loosely, I'm sure she would have given me a couple of out-of-circulation Cypriot pounds and told me to bugger off. To be honest, I don't even think I would have got a couple of quid out of her. I would just get the 'bugger off' end of it! I remembered she had an exceptionally healthy set of lungs on her. Back in the day, when we visited, you could hear her screaming at her kids (my cousins) and my uncle from way down the road in the adjacent village. She could even be heard above the background noise of mating donkeys... she was that loud!

My uncle was my mum's younger brother and was such a great bloke. He would see all, hear all, but would say nothing... he was totally non-judgemental. He had a great strength of character. I would have some fantastic chats with him. He was an honest and true socialist. He was a cross between Jeremy Corbyn and Tony Benn.

There was an occasion when I was around fourteen or fifteen years old, when he backed me up to the detriment of his own son Spiros, who was around eight or nine years old. The fact that he totally doted on him didn't even come into it. I'll tell you what happened, as it will give you an insight into what he was like. Spiros had a really cute crossbreed puppy. I remember thinking at the time that he was absolutely gorgeous. Before you get the wrong idea, I'm talking about the puppy, not my delightful cousin! Anyway, Spiros was throwing the puppy in the air like a rag doll. At one point, he nearly dropped the puppy, but he somehow managed to grab two of the puppy's legs. That's when I heard the poor thing yelp. I immediately ran over, took the puppy from him while he was verbally protesting and trying to hit me. I pushed him away and as I did so, he tripped over a small flowerpot and started shouting like a spoilt brat that had lost his dummy. He was screaming at me, saying that it was his dog and that he could do whatever he wanted to do and that I had no right to stop him. He was deliriously screeching and he was thumping the concrete floor with his fists. You get the picture? He said that he was going to tell his dad, which he did. While he was having his 'entitled' rant, I checked the puppy out to make sure that he hadn't broken anything.

When my uncle got home after work, my cousin went running over to him telling him what had happened. The first thing my uncle did was to ask after the puppy. I said the puppy was fine and added that I couldn't just stand by and watch this poor little creature being treated so badly. It wasn't right. My uncle turned to my cousin and asked him if it was true and after some coaxing, he admitted it was. In the end, Spiros was grounded for the evening and my uncle spent the evening with the puppy. The funny thing about it was that Spiros then went running to my aunt, who backed him up. He was playing both parents off against each another. No wonder he was the way he was... a manipulative nightmare child!

On with the story we go... I was invited in. Everyone else was out and we had a chat about family and things... you know the kind of awkward conversations you have when you haven't seen someone in a long time. During all of this, we ended up munching slices of hard halloumi and sweet red watermelon – a great combination of tastes. You should try it. She asked me what my plans were and if I had somewhere to stay. I said that I hadn't found anywhere yet. She said that I could stay with them as they had the room, which is what I was hoping for and I happily accepted. At least it would be cheap. In fact, it was cheaper than cheap. It was free! She showed me to their guest room and I took out my sleeping bag and laid it on the bed. She immediately took it off the bed and said that she'd wash it for me. She was probably thinking that it was infested with something or other. I wasn't complaining. I could tell from the various expressions on her face that she didn't approve of my current lifestyle living in hostels and the like, looking a bit like a tramp and living off my wits. She would rather see me married to a good old village-type Greek Cypriot girl, have a huge metal chain and padlock around my neck, seventeen kids and that would be my lot.

Once I'd settled in, we went over to the next-door neighbour who had a daughter, whom I'd played with when we were younger. My mum had said to me in the past that there had been some marital interest from her parents for when we were older. Thankfully nothing materialized... it saved me saying, "No chance!" I was not going to the chapel and I was not going to get married!

We knocked on the door and we were greeted by the girl's mother who, yep, you've guessed it, looked me up and down and said with her eyes, "Who the fuck is this?" I noticed a small smile starting to take shape on my aunt's face as she said,

"This is my nephew Niko, Eleni's son".

The look on the neighbour's face was a picture. It was as if a superhero had just rescued her daughter from a 100-foot precipice and flown her to a place of safety. Was it a lucky escape for her or me? Who knows? As it happened, a superhero did rescue her daughter. She was married with two children and lived with her husband under the same roof as her parents. I think it was me who had the lucky escape to be honest. From that moment on, it was the customary nod of disgust from the girl's mother. I thought it was quite funny and so did my mum when I eventually landed on her doorstep and told her.

My uncle came home that afternoon and was pleasantly surprised to see me. He said that he'd spoken to my mum on the phone a couple of weeks ago and she mentioned that I might pop over for a few days but said nothing was certain. It was good to see him and after dinner we went out to the harbour and rang my mum from a public phone box; reversed the charges of course! As I put the phone down, he said that she was a little worried as she hadn't heard from me for over a week. He went on to say that the phone call would probably put her mind at rest.

I bought him a coffee and a pastry and we had a long chat about life and what I had been up to. He surprised me by saying that in a way he regretted not aimlessly travelling. He got married in his early twenties and by that time he'd lost his enthusiasm for travelling. During that evening, as he was talking, he actually reinforced my thoughts on life and that exploring the world was a way to be content and at peace with my own company. He was trying to convince me to go to Czechoslovakia (now known as the Czech Republic) as he'd spent a lot of time living and working there. He absolutely loved it. I hadn't ruled it out but in the words of Queen's *Bohemian Rhapsody*, it was more a case of *'Anywhere the wind blows'*.

The next day I pottered about in the old town of Larnaca, looking around and trying to remember places I'd been to as a child. I found the local bus station with its old and battered diesel vehicles and I bought some fruit from the nearby market. I wandered down to the beach, which was called Finikoudes, which roughly translates into 'palm trees'. It was aptly named as the promenade was and still is lined with palm trees overlooking the sea. I sat on a rock near the harbour eating fruit and looked out to sea with my cute little black and white, furry cat friend, who had just befriended me. He or she was content sitting with me. I have to say that I was already getting bored of Larnaca and just the whole Cyprus thing, so I decided to see when the next ferry was leaving for Rhodes. To my horror, it wasn't for another four days. I could see myself going stir crazy. I bought a ticket for the ferry and pottered around in the medieval fort/castle at the end of the promenade for the rest of the day, which was quite interesting.

I got back to my aunt and uncle's place and noticed that my rucksack had not been closed properly. I was sure that I had tied the straps in my usual manner. Maybe I hadn't. I let the thought pass but as I opened the rucksack, I realised that someone had been through my things. I wasn't too bothered as there was nothing worth taking. As I was putting things back in my own peculiar way, my aunt came into the room, and looked at the small collection of unwashed and rather pungent clothes on the floor. As luck would have it, she insisted that she should wash them. Funnily enough I was actually thinking of washing them myself. Again, I wasn't going to argue. It was fine with me. They had a washing machine, which was handy. Was that the individual who had been rifling through my bag trying to make amends after being potentially caught out? Absolutely, yes! To be honest, the noxious fumes that were escaping from my rucksack were definitely a nasty nasal experience to those who worshipped the god of cleanliness.

That evening, we all went to visit my cousin Lenia, who had moved out with her husband. She was having a family and friends' get-together. All my uncle's children and grandchildren were there. It had rained heavily a few hours beforehand and my uncle went to pick some snails from the fields to take over to my cousin. There were quite a few people there. The BBQ coals were hot and cooking away when we got there. There were all the customary greetings which included, "What the fuck are you doing bumming around?" and "Why aren't you married yet?" These were their typical traditional and blinkered views. You get the idea! My uncle stood by laughing but he knew exactly where I was coming from. He understood. It was actually strangely nice to see them and we had some good chats in my broken London Greek dialect and their broken English.

The next day, I caught a bus to a place called Ayia Napa. Apparently, it was once a quaint little fishing village with its unspoilt sandy beaches, resident monks and monastery. I have to say it's no longer so quaint, especially when developers moved in to make quite a few quid here and there. With that in mind, I had a long walk along the beach and then on to the monastery. Unfortunately, the monastery was closed to visitors for the day, so I started to make my way back to the beach as there wasn't much else there.

On the way back I saw an old man dressed in the traditional Cypriot way. By that I mean that he was wearing a white shirt, a black waistcoat and a black 'vraka'. A vraka is a pair of loose-fitting trousers that look as if they have been wrapped around like a nappy. An ideal dress code for those who have a certain fetish!

I'm digressing again! Anyway, he was leaning over some railings. He was crying and slapping the railings. I went over to him and asked him, in the best Greek I could muster, if he was okay. He nodded and then proceeded to launch into a tirade of abuse at the enormous crater and mechanical digger just the other side of the safety railings, which I might add, were not very secure. I had the feeling that health and safety didn't feature very high on the Cypriot agenda. The old man was in tears saying:

"They are ruining my village. I've lived here all my life, as have my parents and grandparents. I was married here, brought up my children here and now we have this!"

He was pointing at the large earthy hole. He went on to say that this was going to be an underground night club and probably the first of many. Before he walked away with his stick, he said it was the beginning of the end. It was a very apocalyptic comment, but I totally understood him. People don't generally like change, especially if it's somewhere that you've grown up and have had some good memories. I genuinely felt sorry for him. I stood there for a while, thinking about how many other sleepy villages were going to be transformed into an environment of screeching, scantily clad, chaotic individuals mixed in with screaming police sirens. I suppose that's what some people call progress!

That evening, I was chatting to my aunt and I told her about the old man and she understood how he felt. I would think most of the older generation would think like that; watching the village they grew up in change into something unrecognisable. As we were talking, my uncle came home from work looking hot and tired, as he was on his feet for most of the day. He was a popular barber in the middle of the market area by the local bus station. He'd literally crossed the door frame of the kitchen, when my aunt demanded he should do some jobs around the house. He was a quiet man and was not going to get drawn into an argument. He simply said to her that there are ways of talking to people and asking for things to be done, without shouting out demands... good for him!

Now, where is all this going, I hear you ask. Just have some patience and I'll tell you. My uncle turned to me and quietly said, "Come with me, there's something I want to show you." With the backdrop of my aunt ranting like a gaggling banshee, we jumped onto my uncle's motorbike. Close your eyes and picture the scene - the neighbours hanging out of windows, mouths drooling and making exaggerated mental notes for tomorrow morning's local coffee, cake and gossip session.

We were heading for the harbour where my uncle had a small boat. He would often go night fishing to get away from everything; and who can blame him? I suppose it was his open-air man cave. We had a bite to eat, a few bottles of Keo beer and headed out into the dark void we call the night sea. He wanted me to see Larnaca's lights from the sea. It was the most bizarre experience, especially after downing a few bottles of the amber nectar. We were a fair way out and we chatted some more about my mum, his life and my grandparents, while casting nets with the not-so-full moon hanging around and shimmering on the water around us. He didn't mention my aunt once. I was very curious about her background. I wanted to know if she was always so loud and demanding, but I thought it best to keep my nose out of it. Thinking back to the times when we used to customarily visit them, as if there was no other place on earth to go during our summer holidays - I have memories of my cousins being shouty and waddling around like penguins. They obviously took the lead from my aunt. Anyway, regarding my aunt, I thought I'd best save that conversation for my return home with my mum.

My uncle asked me if I wanted to see my half-brother who lived not too far from Larnaca. At the time he worked as a translator on a nearby British base. I thought that it might be a good thing to do, but given the non-history between us, I decided against it. In a nutshell, my mum had met and married his dad and had given birth to two boys and a girl by the age of around twenty-one. The oldest was about 5 years old. So, to put you in the picture, I have three half-blood siblings and a full-blood brother. My half siblings' dad was a supporter of the growing communist party in Cyprus at the time. It was said that he openly and very strongly supported them. Some of the villagers were not happy with what he was preaching and decided to frame him. I'm not exactly sure how these villagers managed to plant a hand gun in my mum's house/shack, which was apparently a small, two-room, mud brick building backing onto a field. The police were informed that my mum's husband had a gun and he was consequently arrested and thrown into jail.

During his time in jail, my mum's in-laws forcibly took the children from my mum, stating a whole catalogue of reasons, none of which were true. The law in those days was heavily weighted against women and more in favour of the men. Women's rights were extremely minimal. My mum pleaded to have her children back. She managed to get one of her children back. My full-blood brother and I grew up with him. As Cyprus was a Crown colony during this period, my mum decided to go to England in 1952/53 by ship, which was paid for by my grandparents. My mum obviously felt guilty and devastated about leaving her two other children behind, but in reality she had no choice.

As the years went by, she tried to make amends with my half-brother and sister, who had been told all sorts of derogatory things about her. We eventually started seeing them, but it was very, very rocky at first. I had built up a healthy relationship with my half-sister, as had my mum, and we saw her quite regularly. Regarding my half-brother, it was a different case. It became quite a challenging situation, especially with his wife, and it didn't quite work out for us. At the time I felt very sorry for my mum… I still feel sorry for her to this day.

I often remembered feeling a heavy heart whenever my mum spoke about what had happened back in the day. It must have been extremely traumatic for both my mum and my half-siblings. It's definitely something I would not have wanted to experience. My mum's and my half-siblings' dilemma is just one case among millions, who have experienced similar, if not worse situations. If you remember at the beginning of the book, I spoke about people travelling to places for various reasons. In my mum's case, she was travelling to get away from a major crisis in her young life, which she had absolutely no control over. She wanted to kick start her life again in England. She stayed with one of her sisters and her husband, who were able to get her a job to pay for her keep.

Once again, I've gone off track but now I'll continue with what I was saying. Anyway, my uncle and I got back in the early hours of the morning and we tiptoed into the house like a couple of thieves, trying not to wake the snoring Smaug! I was very impressed with our stealthy movements. There was no noise at all. Once in bed, I fell asleep almost immediately, only to wake up a little while later with an enormous urge. No! No! No! Stop right there! It's not that sort of urge! I can see the direction your mind's taking! Now will you please let me finish the sentence! As I was saying earlier, I woke up a little while later with an enormous urge to relieve my bladder. It must have been all those beers. As it happens, the toilet was at the far end of the garden. My penance for drinking so much was to drag myself to the little brick cubicle, to quickly and quietly make my amber delivery. Alas, I have to report that I couldn't quite hold it in and in a nutshell, I embarrassingly ended up partially wetting myself. I might add that it was the first and last time it has ever happened as an adult.

To be fair, it wasn't too bad as I managed to halt the majority of the oncoming tsunami.

Under the smirking gaze of the man in the moon, the second part of this little mishap was to get rid of the evidence as quickly and quietly as possible. After all, I didn't want to get found out now, did I? My plan was to hide my M&S specials. There were some large pots that were all closely positioned near to the window of the room where I was sleeping. I shoved the garment in between the pots and washed myself down like one would. Once all that was done, I crawled back into bed and slept well, only to wake up early thinking about the previous night. No one was up, so I took the opportunity to have a shower before everyone else. I quickly grabbed my pants from behind the pots and while having a shower, I washed them along with a couple of t-shirts to make it look authentic and hung them out to dry.

Just after I'd finished, my aunt came into the room and apologised for my uncle's behaviour (really!) She asked me where we went last night. I told her what we did as it wasn't really a secret. She then asked me to remind her when I was leaving. Obviously, she couldn't wait to get rid of me, which was perfectly understandable. I answered by saying that the ferry was leaving the evening after tomorrow, so I would be leaving mid-morning. I spent the next couple of days walking, reading and people watching.

In my view, getting off the island couldn't come quick enough. Being stuck in the middle of people having countless domestics was certainly not my idea of fun. That included my cousin Thekla (named after my grandmother) her husband and their little girl, who were also living there. Their child, whose name I can't remember for the life of me, can only be described as a collection of all the overindulged children in *Willy Wonka and the Chocolate Factory*, rolled into one. That's no exaggeration! I then had to contend with the antics of my cousin's alpha male husband who was only concerned with his own self-importance. His stock phase was, "How long is dinner going to be?" and he kept going on about how he stood to inherit my uncle's house. In my opinion, the only thing he should inherit would be a secure cell in a hospital. He needed some serious help!

Before I left to catch the ferry to Rhodes, I said my piece to him in front of my aunt, uncle and my cousin. Just for your information, my uncle had four children. Three of them had flown the nest, which meant I had to put up with my cousin and her arsehole of a husband. As I laid into him, my aunt and uncle didn't say a word. My cousin's husband was none too pleased but that wasn't my problem...

it was his! I thanked my aunt and uncle for everything. As I got into the service taxi to go to Limassol they both said, "Well done, he's had that coming for a long time". At least my outburst united them for a little while. Thinking about it, were they just putting up with him or were they scared of him? I'll never know...

RHODES

No disrespect to my aunt and uncle, but it felt good to be on the road again, having the freedom to do what I wanted to do without being questioned about it. I have to say that it wasn't my uncle. It was everyone else around me. I felt that by their blinkered views, I was being unintentionally restricted. I don't think that they meant to make me feel like that in any way. I just think they were living the life that was expected of them and they assumed everyone else would have the same values in that respect.

Some years later my uncle and my aunt divorced and my uncle ended up in Swansea of all places. We'd often go and see him there with his partner and he would often visit and stay with my mum. The conversations we would have were brilliant. He brought up my parting gift to his son-in-law in front of my mum. My mum congratulated me and added that she'd never liked him. We were all in agreement on that!

Anyway, I got to Limassol and pottered about with my rucksack and my recently washed and sundried pants. I sat around various places reading. I chatted to some old men in one of those Greek Cypriot cafés, as best as I could, in my London Greek. I found these guys quite funny. They couldn't get over the fact that I was living out of my rucksack with no job and *No Particular Place to Go* – a great Chuck Berry song. They were going on about how their sons and daughters were all married, had children, how they had massive houses and drove around in great big, dirty Mercs and BMWs. In a way, I couldn't help feeling sorry for them. I found it interesting that they didn't mention the fact that they were all probably mortgaged up and in debt up to their eyeballs. It was in complete contrast to what I wanted and what I was doing. They really couldn't get their heads around it. It was totally alien to them. I actually enjoyed the fact that they were struggling with the concept.

About mid to late afternoon, I made my way to the port, negotiated passport control, the token security guards and boarded the ferry. Yep! You've guessed it again. It was deck class and a spot around the perimeter of the boat was my home for the next eighteen hours or so. Why change a system that works? This journey was around six hours longer than the one between Haifa and Limassol. I stood on the deck like a meerkat, watching people stumbling along the quayside with their huge, four-wheeled suitcases. It was very obvious by their suitcases and travel attire that they were not going to keep us company on deck. It was quite amusing to watch, though. You might agree or you might not agree with me regarding the next few sentences. From my perspective, the situation lent itself into them and us... it was unquestionably a case of snobbery on both sides of the fence. They wouldn't want to associate themselves with us. We were the great unwashed! When you flip the coin, it was inverted snobbery on our behalf. We wouldn't really want to associate ourselves with them. All this is a figure of speech. I'm obviously speaking on behalf of myself when I talk about not wanting to associate with their lifestyle. Then there were those who would tentatively cross over and dip their toes into our world! When you get to the ferry crossing from Rhodes to Piraeus, you'll hopefully see what I'm rattling on about. It was an interesting state of affairs really. At the end of the day we are all different. We all have different views, needs and expectations.

During this particular ferry journey, I bedded down next to a small group of strapping young Israeli women. It turns out that they had finished their conscripted term and were on their way to Athens to let their hair down, so to speak. As part of their training, they would strategically learn how to defend themselves. This peculiar little group were trained as medics. I don't remember much about the evening as I shared their water, or what I initially thought was water. They had vodka and gin in clear water bottles and quite honestly, it was like Christmas and Rosh Hashanah simultaneously coming early!

As we ate, drank and slowly lost the will to be polite, they were talking to me about how they were taught to dish out injections in a collective manner. It was definitely not the way I would have wanted to learn how to administer jabs! As part of the initiation process into the *Women in Uniform* class of 1987 (such a great honour and a great Iron Maiden song as well as I've already mentioned) they formed a small circle and invited me to crouch with them. The circle went clockwise and we had to face away from the person behind us. Luckily, there were no needles involved, just the pinching each other's bums, as we went around the circle. You have to bear in mind that we did have quite a bit to drink. It started with a squeal from the other side of the circle and quickly made its way to me. The girl behind me pinched both buttocks and then reached under and momentarily grappled my unsuspecting nadgers, which involved a rather swift World War 2, Panzer division pincer movement. It was very impressive and I have to say that there were definitely no complaints from me on that score.

When all the jollity had died down, the girls explained that in their training, they all sat on chairs in a circle of about eight to ten people who were armed with syringes, which contained immunisations of some sort. It started with one person jabbing the person in front of them. When that was done, the person who had been jabbed would insert his or her needle into the person's arm in front of them, and so on. I can think of better bonding activities, preferably ones that don't involve needles!

After enduring some strange looks from our fellow deck-class buddies, it all settled down and we chatted well into the night about all sorts of things, which ranged from politics to how to tie shoelaces with one hand. That would be a party trick, for sure! I really couldn't imagine these girls being involved in policing and armed combat but Israel being what it is I suppose it's a necessity to have everyone on board.

One of the topics we spoke about was National Service, and how the Orthodox Jewish Community were exempt from serving in the military. The reason for their exemption was that they could study and preserve the sacred Jewish knowledge and traditions, following the Holocaust. In saying this, there are a couple of Orthodox Jewish groups that are opposed to the formation of the State of Israel. They believe that it is an anti-messianic act which has been conceived and born from sin. In short, they believe that they have to wait for heavenly intervention and not the human intervention which led to the formation of the State of Israel in 1948. It's very deep, so I suggest that if you're interested, then use the web to get more information. It really is quite interesting. Mind you, with that said, I suppose its fine to throw rocks at people who have a different view on life etc. It really is a *Mad, Mad, Mad, Mad World* (it's totally unrelated but the title sums it all up. Incidentally, I absolutely love this film). It kind of reminds me of the cartoon *Wacky Races* with Dick Dastardly and Muttley.

Meanwhile, back on deck, human chatter was beginning to fall silent. The only noise to be heard above the snoring and the releasing of noxious fumes into the night air was the ship's throbbing engines doing their duty by getting us to Rhodes. Daylight it seems came early, too early, and I was woken by something crawling over my face. It turned out to be one of the girls, who was trying to wake me up by running her hair over my sticky, salty face and gently trying to inspire some life into me. She wanted me to enjoy the sunrise with her.

As we stood leaning over the side of the ship, we spoke about how serene and beautiful the sunrises were in the middle of the sea and once again, we were not disappointed! While the deck still resembled the aftermath of a wild party, with various pieces of unwashed underwear precariously hanging from the ship's funnel, we witnessed the most amazing stripes of golden light. The light seemed to be entering an endless world of darkness in slow motion. Like I've said before, the beauty of our planet never, ever disappoints me. Yet, there are some complete head cases who want to take this stunning planet away from us, all for the sake of their insecurities, money and power.

After a shared breakfast, visits to the rancid toilets and chats with my new shipmates, we finally docked at Rhodes' Mandraki Harbour. It is said that the entrance to the port had once been straddled by the Colossus of Rhodes. Apparently, this was an enormous bronze statue of the sun god Helios, which was one of the Seven Wonders of the Ancient World. It is said to have been built to thank the gods for the victory following a long siege of Rhodes around 305 BC. According to Pliny the Elder, who was a Roman author, the statue stood thirty-three metres high and took twelve years to construct. Unfortunately, an earthquake around 225 BC toppled the Colossus into the sea. However, modern-day historians dispute the location of the Colossus at the mouth of Mandraki Harbour due to the width of the harbour mouth. They believe that it was erected at a nearby alternative location. Some say that it was at a different harbour, while others say that it stood on a hill overlooking the bay. From a totally classical and romantic view, I would have loved the statue to have a foot on each side of Mandraki Harbour, just like in the pictures. With all this said, I was trying to imagine this massive achievement greeting us as we entered the harbour under the midday sun. My only question would be whether the Colossus was wearing a pair of classical Y-fronts. Or could it be that the statue was baring its tackle to all and sundry? I would imagine it was the latter. What do you think?

The ferry was to be moored up for a couple hours, so to my surprise my sunrise buddy escorted me off our host for the past eighteen hours. She was given a pass off the boat and into Rhodes Town, which was only a stone's throw away from the harbour. We walked into Rhodes Town. It was really very picturesque. We meandered into a square with a stone water fountain in the middle of it. She sat me down on the base of some stone steps and went off and bought two cans of coke and two packets of crisps. I protested but I quickly gave in as she shot me one of those 'take them' looks.

Anyway, we chatted about various things, including life as we knew it, until it was time for her to go back to the ferry to continue her journey onto Athens. As we said our goodbyes, she let it slip that she was entertaining the idea of getting off at Rhodes with me. I was flattered. In one respect it would have been a pleasant interlude, but I'm glad she decided to stick to her original plans. No disrespect meant, but I wanted to be on my own, to do what I wanted to do and not think about anyone else. So, like I said, we eventually said our goodbyes and I watched her walk along the harbour and get back onto the ferry from an arch in the Old Town walls. Once she was safely on board, I decided to find somewhere to stay.

My sole intention was to find a bed for a few nights. Nothing else interested me until I had achieved that. I knocked on the first place I saw, which had a very shabby pair of tall, light blue doors with a metal knocker on each door. I was just about able to reach them if I stood on a triple extension ladder. Above the door was a piece of what could only be mistaken for driftwood with the word, 'Pensione' haphazardly painted in black. I had my suspicions that it was possibly written by a toddler. Obviously, not a Greek toddler otherwise it would read, 'πανσιόν'. Then again, it could have been the infamous Lydia, the multi-lingual and multi-talented toddler who had written forty-eight books in different languages by the age of two!

Sorry about that; I'm going off-piste again. Let's get back on track to securing a bed, a room or even an air-conditioned hut. So once I had mastered the pair of grand knockers, a well-dressed, middle-aged lady, with long, black, curly hair opened the door. I spoke to her in Greek as I thought it would be the polite thing to do. It's the 'When in Rome' syndrome kicking in! I asked her if she had a bed, a room or anything resembling somewhere to sleep for a few nights. It was obvious that she was trying not to break into fits of laughter and asked me if I spoke English. In my best Queen's or should I say, my best King's English, I said that I did. The lady replied by saying that it was a good thing that I spoke English, otherwise we would probably be standing on the doorstep till next week trying to figure out what I wanted. She went on to say, "Stick to English. Your Greek is terrible!"

With all the formalities and the one-way insults over (which was fine) she informed me that there were no rooms available as such. However, there was an attic which led onto a flat roof, if I was interested. It would cost me one hundred Drachmas a night, (somewhere equivalent to fifty pence a night) and that included a basic breakfast of tea or coffee and toast but as time went on, I would get an egg thrown in. The price was definitely up my street, so I accepted it straight away without even having a look.

She then let me in and we sat around a well-worn wooden table alongside an older man and another woman around my age. It turns out that the man was her husband and the girl was her daughter. I was offered a coffee, which was welcome, and we spoke in English, which was handy. She took down my particulars. Steady tiger! By that I meant my name and passport number and I was given a key to the front door. I was informed of the rules, regarding the communal showers, toilets, breakfast times, no room jumping etc.

On the surface, it felt very homely, welcoming and relaxed, and I have to say it was! I was shown the penthouse suite. The attic had a light switch, a bulb, various types of dust and whatever lurked in the shadows where the light was unable to penetrate. It was exactly as I was told; extremely basic. No bed! No nothing! All there was in terms of furniture were some bits of broken tables and chairs. You've obviously heard about an elephant's graveyard? Well this was a table and chair graveyard. Luxury at its best! Mind you, I shouldn't complain at fifty pence per night with breakfast. In saying that, once I got onto the flat roof, the skyline of Rhodes Town was fantastic, especially at night. It was well worth fifty pence and more besides.

I lay my sleeping bag down on an old duvet which I had found, which I dusted down on the flat roof. I have to say it was very comfortable. I made the place my own. Once I had settled in, I decided to potter about and explore the immediate area. On the way out, I bumped into the owner's daughter Katerina. She was also on her way out, clutching a well-used, medium-sized holdall. With an amused look on her face, she asked me if I liked my room. What else could I say apart from, "I feel blessed!" We walked out together and I shut the giant doors behind us. We walked back down towards the old stone fountain, chatting away. She said that she had noticed me and a girl laughing on the steps earlier. I apologised for having a good time (like one does) and she said that apart from the noise that we were making, she noticed how scruffy we both looked. Scruffy? Us? Me? I couldn't agree more and quite honestly, I loved it. I was most certainly beginning to warm to Katerina's sense of humour, whereas I could imagine that other people would probably find her offensive.

She was on her way to a karate class, which was situated outside the Old Town walls in the modern part of the town; hence the holdall. As a matter of course, she let me know that she had just gained her brown belt, which I was pretty impressed with. I then let her know that I had been to karate classes and had got to a green belt. I jokingly animated a very rubbish karate kata, saying that we should spar one day. She replied by holding both my hands up, saying that she would probably beat the crap out of me. We both nodded, knowing full well that would be the case. We spoke about full and partial contact in martial art sports and how in one respect full contact was good, but could be extremely dangerous. I found that out when I started to learn Wing-Chung many years later, which is full contact. I lasted about a month after being battered and bruised after each session. It was not for me! We said we'd catch up for a drink later and off we went in our respective directions.

I just literally walked around looking for cheaper than cheap food establishments. I have to say there were hardly any cheap places in this particular tourist trap. I came across Greece's typical takeaway food... the gyro. Again, this would be my staple diet but the prices within the Old Town were geared up for tourists. However, I did have the very occasional stuffed pepper and huge stuffed tomato, which were delicious and decorated with charcoal! They did taste good, though. I often ate outside the Old Town. The new and modern Rhodean metropolis was generally much cheaper and it was where the locals would congregate. It's always good to eat where the locals eat. It's generally cheaper and there is no pretence, unless you eat in an overpriced and pretentiously hollow cafe. As a side issue, have you noticed how the good old workman cafes are gradually disappearing, only to be replaced by these overpriced, la-di-da places?

Anyway, historically Rhodes Old Town seemed fascinating. There were lots of buildings and narrow cobbled streets, with some supporting arches separating and holding up the buildings across the side-streets. All this was mixed in with some residents' washed smalls dripping on any unsuspecting tourists below. Lovely! The large ornate doors laden with bright colours caught my eye. The buildings had shuttered windows and well-tended window boxes with their obligatory cracks in the walls, crying out to be plastered over; very picturesque. It's the stuff that postcards are made of. It looked and felt a little bit like the Old City of Jerusalem, but on a smaller scale.

I felt very at home. I spent the rest of the day reading and walking around... it was perfection. Unlike Jerusalem, Rhodes didn't have that nervous energy feeling. Don't get me wrong, I loved and still love Jerusalem but in comparison, Rhodes Town was totally relaxed and it seemed like a place without major incidents.

I got back to the Pensione, used my newly acquired key to let myself in and began looking at a couple of maps on the wall. There was one of Rhodes Town and another one of Rhodes Island. As I was looking at the well-fingered maps, Sophia (Katerina's mother) emerged from one of the side rooms. We got talking about how long I was going to stay on Rhodes and places to see around the island. She recommended a place on Rhodes' southern tip called Prasonisi. This was a place where two seas meet. Sophia described it as one of nature's amazing sights and said it took approximately one-and-a-half hours to two hours to get there by bus. She also recommended the beautiful village of Lindos, among other places. I had heard from other fellow travellers that during the day, on the approach to Lindos, the sun beats down on the white-painted buildings, almost blinding you with its reflection. Others had mentioned the lovely tranquil nights, when the stars twinkle in the darkness to the backdrop of the vocal sea waves. Sophia spoke about a structure overlooking the village. She said that sitting like a crown, was Lindos' Acropolis, which was perched on a cliff, protecting its residents. Sophia told me that Lindos wasn't as far as Prasonisi, which was handy. I toyed with the idea that I could maybe do the two in one day. If not, I could break the journey up and I could no doubt find a remote beach or something to sleep on. The choice was mine. To be honest, there really was no rush to do both in one day.

As we were talking, a few people came in and went straight to their rooms. They weren't very sociable... but hey, that's how some people are. I decided to practically inspect the communal showers and toilets. They were clean and they had hot water, which was a bonus! I hadn't had a shower for a good few days. While on the ferry, my skin had developed a kind of stickiness from the salty sea air. With that said, I performed my cleanliness duties and retired to my humble abode at the top of my little world in a very contented state of mind. I was too tired to meet up with Katerina, so I stayed in my sleeping bag.

I slept the whole night without any interruptions. It was very peaceful. I hadn't realised how tired I was. Breakfast was great... tea, coffee and toast. The whole process took around two hours. As always, I was talking to people and gaining information and exchanging stories. Again, some were sociable and others not so much. Sophia asked me (sporting a big cheeky smile on her face) if I wanted my penthouse suite cleaned. I could see where Katerina got her sense of humour from. You can imagine my response, which of course, as always, was tongue in cheek.

Katerina was in and out of the main room, picking plates up and generally cleaning. She eventually sat down with a big cup of steaming hot coffee in a tacky mug sporting the words, 'Idyllic Rhodes'. Plastered on the side of the mug was a postcard-type picture of the Colossus straddling the harbour, just like in the good old days! She must have seen my reaction as I looked at her, then the mug and then back at her, with an amusing look of disgust starting to emerge on my face. Her response was a playful Basil Fawlty slap around the back of my head accompanied with the words, "Don't say a word... reh malaka". If you don't know what 'malaka' means then I would advise you to look it up, especially as you have the whole world at your fingertips. The word itself is widely used in the Greek community and has two meanings. One is meant in a friendly way and one is obviously not! I'll let you decide which one Katerina meant!

Anyway, after the physical abuse had been administered, she asked me what my plans were for the day. To be honest, I didn't have any so she asked me if I wanted to hang out with her. She would show me around Rhodes Town (old and new) have lunch, etc., and if I wanted, I could pop along to her karate session later on. Did I? I certainly did!

Katerina was great company and she knew a little something about everything. However, she said she had to finish cleaning the kitchen and the main communal areas, which included the toilets and showers. She cheekily said, "You can help out if you want". I replied by saying that I had to consult my agent first which earned me a push onto one of the sofas. With my hands over my face I shouted, "Entaxei! Entaxei!" Google time again! "OK... I'll do it! I'll do it! Just don't hurt me!" At that point, Sophia came running out of the kitchen wondering what all the noise was about. Katerina said that she had convinced me to help her clean up. Sophia laughed and gave Katerina the thumbs-up. Sophia went on to say, "If he does a good job, he can have the Penthouse Suite for free... he can earn his keep!" I didn't need any encouraging. I was more than happy to do it.

It didn't take very long and after being accepted as an official member of the workforce, we wandered off into Rhodes Town. She showed me a dry gravel/mud-covered square in the New Town which was like stepping back in time. It was great. There were cafés with weary-looking tables accompanied by old, sun-bleached, rush-seated chairs that left an imprint on the back of your legs. They were so rickety that they were ready to collapse; similar to the ones my grandparents had. The chairs and tables were situated in the middle of the square. They were overlooked by artistically designed pigeon droppings, which were delicately and lovingly arranged on the overhead canvas canopy. The canopy shielded loads of food stalls from the weather (not very hygienic, I know) but I suppose it added to the taste. It's not everyone's cup of tea, but to me, it was heaven on earth. It was a good place to sit and watch people, which I often did. Katerina introduced me to a couple of her friends that worked on a food stall, where I would often get free soft drinks and the occasional shot of Ouzo or Raki, when their boss wasn't around.

It turned out to be a good day. We chatted and walked around for hours and eventually ended up at Katerina's karate club. On this occasion, I sat and watched which was interesting as it was all in Greek. I have to admit, I found it quite difficult to follow. Katerina trained almost every day and she managed to convince the instructor to let me do a couple of session for free. I have to say that I got back into it almost seamlessly. I decided that when I eventually got back to where I was escaping from, I would check out a few clubs!

That evening we borrowed a bottle of whisky from Katerina's dad's vast collection. He had loads of them in every crevice of his store room and Katerina assured me he wouldn't miss it. We joked that he was accumulating the alcohol for her wedding... as Greek dads do! I'm in no way, shape or form talking about weddings here. God forbid! However, if I translate the whisky collection into music, I have so many vinyl records, CDs and cassette tapes that I don't really know what I have and I probably wouldn't miss one or two going missing! Well, to be honest, I would notice and I have noticed. On one occasion while I was away, my mum needed some card to design a clothing garment. As it happens, she didn't have any card knocking about, so she went digging around in my record collection and pulled out my treasured Ramones *Rocket to Russia* album. The album itself and the outer cover were intact but the inner sleeve (made of card) was missing. My mum sheepishly owned up to it but I couldn't be angry with her for long... she's my mum. However, it was such a brilliant inner sleeve design. The sleeve had lyrics and little animations depicting each song. For some time afterwards, I was in mourning every time I played it. On another occasion, I was looking for a certain Elvis Presley album called *From Elvis in Memphis* which I wanted to play. As I searched for it, I noticed that not only could I not find that particular album, but I couldn't see many of the other Elvis Presley albums that I had. I never did find out what happened to those albums. My mum had no idea what happened to them. To this day I still don't know what happened to them.

So, coming back on track with Katerina's dad's bottle of whisky, I was sure that her dad would notice, but as far as I knew, he never directly let on. I never really heard anything to the contrary. Anyway, armed with a bottle of whisky, water and cans of coke, we went onto the rooftop next to my Penthouse Suite and slowly but surely got sozzled. Needless to say, next morning's cleaning chores were somewhat challenging for me. Alcohol and I have never really seen eye to eye. I was pretty much wiped out the next day! Katerina, on the other hand, was fine. It's alright for some. Lucky cow! She was one of these people that would get pissed but was fine the following morning. Like I said, lucky cow!

That morning, I planned to go to Lindos by bus, which stopped quite frequently to pick up and drop people off. Bearing in mind I felt rough, it was actually a good journey considering the driver was dodging the odd pothole here and there. As the bus was approaching Lindos, the road became remarkably better. I assumed this because we, the passengers, were not holding on for dear life and making the sign of the cross every five seconds. Taking everything into account which included the potholes, air conditioning and the state of my head, the journey passed without incident.

The view of Lindos from the road was amazing, just as Sophia and others had said. The sun's reflection beating down onto the whitewashed buildings was something else. It doesn't matter how much you're told about something, you can't really appreciate it until you've seen it with your own eyes. Sometimes you're amazed by what you see. Other times, you think it's alright but nothing special. Personally, at this point, I was in awe for a few seconds. It was definitely one of those moments.

This is a strange connection and you'll probably agree, but it reminded me of someone I went to school with called Daryl. He mentioned to me that his dad was the bass player in sixties group, The Dave Clark Five. Obviously, I was sceptical at the time. I couldn't get the instant information I needed by looking it up online. The internet wasn't even a twinkle in Tim Berners-Lee's eye in those days. I ended up asking one of his best friends, Peter and he said it was true. I still thought that it was a wind-up. Walking home from school that afternoon I had one of those light-bulb moments. My brother had one of those *K-Tel* various artist albums. One of The Dave Clark Five's tracks was on it. It was called *Glad All Over* and I remembered seeing a circle with a picture of the band inside it. Incidentally, I played that album to death and funnily enough, I still have the album. It was non-verbally handed down to me when my brother moved out. Anyway, the photo was quite small. The second I got home, I ran to this enormous dresser we had and in between saying a quick hello to my mum, I slid the doors open which housed our records. I found the album and looked at the picture of the band. It was too small to make out the band's faces. Using a magnifying glass, I went over each face meticulously. There was definitely a likeness with one of the band members and Daryl. When I realised it was true, it became one of those incredible moments for me. The next day at school I asked Daryl so many questions about the band and his dad. I remember thinking at the time that I hoped he thought I wasn't being a pain. I was just interested; that's all it was really. The only other thing I remembered about Daryl was that he used to eat whole raw onions, just like you would eat an apple, in the playground. Strange but true!

Anyway, after getting over my blinding introduction to the sacred white walls of Lindos, the bus pulled up and spluttered to a halt. It sounded as if the radiator was about to explode. It stopped into what I can only describe as a typical Greek bus station made for a couple of buses. To be honest, I wouldn't describe it as a station, more of a glorified bus stop. It had a few tourist stalls selling snacks and your typical souvenir tat. I jumped off the bus and started following my fellow bus commuters into Lindos. My first impression as I started walking around was that Lindos was clean and stunningly beautiful, with its spotless white buildings and their plain-coloured shutters and doors. It was somewhat similar to the backstreets in Rhodes Town. The only difference between the two, were the white buildings. The people that lived here took great pride in their town and must have regularly painted the buildings.

I wandered around as usual just taking it in. I noticed that there were a couple of donkeys tied up. I felt sorry for them as they were obviously being used as tourist fodder. I bought some apples for myself and for the donkeys. I sat around munching and watched people going about their day. There were lots of restaurants with waiters and waitresses (Ah, The Waitresses...now that was a great band. They did a great Christmas song... check them out) doing their best to entice any stray, unsuspecting tourist. Understandably, by the way I was dressed they didn't pay much attention to me. I didn't look like a tourist with money so I wasn't approached. It actually suited me. I had similar experiences with the cafés but not as much.

However, in the countless souvenir shops that were spread all over the town, like a rash, I was followed around like a known criminal. Isn't it interesting that we are all judged by how we dress and present ourselves? I suppose we all have prejudices of sorts. In one particular souvenir shop, a man and women (the shop owners) challenged me in front of other customers. They asked to look in my bag as they thought I had stolen something. I was told that I was seen putting my hand in my bag. I have to say it was fair enough. I emptied my tattered munitions bag on the table. At the same time, I explained that I often put my hand into my bag to check that I had everything and that I hadn't been pickpocketed. I added that the feeling worked both ways in terms of suspicions. When they realised that they had misjudged me, they were very apologetic, adding that they'd had lots of stock go missing. I actually said that even well-dressed people steal things. They understood what I was getting at and they once again apologised.

I got the feeling from the other customers in the shop that they were most disappointed that I was telling the truth and that the police were not called, which would ultimately end up culminating in a street battle and a siege around the shop. I suppose it would have been exciting and something to write on their postcards apart from, 'Wish you were here', which they probably didn't mean. However, going back to the shop owners, they tactfully commented on how bad my Greek was (there was a definite theme emerging here) made me a coffee and we had a good chat about things... in English. I have to say that after the initial exchange, it was really quite pleasant and enjoyable. They were decent people.

I left the shop and decided to wander around taking in more of the same... more restaurants, more cafés and more souvenir shops. As lovely as Lindos was, I decided to walk down to the beach, which wasn't that far. It was fairly busy, taking into account that the temperatures were starting to drop. I took off my plimsolls and walked along the beach, immersing my feet in the clear, turquoise coloured sea water.

I trudged the whole length of the bay and sat down on the sand with my back on an uncomfortable rock to read my latest acquisition... a Mills and Boon book no less. It was a book that I had swapped. That's how I got my books... I swapped them. I'm not sure if I would be able to swap this particular book that easily, though. I made sure that I hid the cover from any prying eyes. I couldn't really be seen with it. It wouldn't do my street credibility any favours now, would it? It was definitely not the type of genre I would normally choose to read but I have to say it was a strange but interesting read. It was set in Romania with an unexpected twist at the end. Secretly, it was a good, easy read and I actually enjoyed it! I can't believe I actually said that! I know, I know! It's a shocking thing to admit to but I can now tick it off my book bucket list. That's the only thing I'm going to say about it, so keep it quiet! The less information about this entr'acte getting out into the universe, the better!

After some time just chilling out, I walked back along the beach to another smaller bay and sat under a tree away from the beach, enjoying the view and the sea breeze. It was idyllic. I felt very at peace with myself. I very briefly entertained the thought of what was happening back home and reminded myself to ring my mum; reverse charges of course!

Just above me on the hill overlooking Lindos, was and still is, their own Acropolis. I decided to go up and have a look and take in the view of Lindos and the surrounding area. Once there, I was quite impressed with what greeted me and what had survived over the years. I always find it amazing how these structures have survived time and nature's own wrath. I stayed up on the Acropolis and watched the sunset with three other tourists, who turned out to be Italian. They were respectfully turned out with their branded items and were staying in a decent hotel somewhere down near the beach. I was going to tell them about my own personal rooftop penthouse with amazing views overlooking Rhodes Town. However, I thought it best not tell them just in case they thought they had overpaid for a bit of luxury and tried to mug me for my keys. After all, not everyone gets to pay fifty pence for dust, broken furniture, slaps and two karate lessons! I didn't want them to feel hard done by. I try to be sensitive to other people's feelings... I'm good like that. Excuse me... I need a sick bag!

Anyway, we were the only people up there... it was our own personal audience with the sunset. What a truly magnificent sight. We watched the sun lower itself bit by bit onto the horizon. It effortlessly created various blends of orange and red onto the sea and into the surrounding sky, until it finally dropped below the horizon. The sun and the moon had changed places without any hint of chaos or fuss. I stayed up on the hill a little longer after everyone had left. It was truly peaceful apart from the low muffled noise down in the village, and the crickets (not Buddy Holly's Crickets) having the time of their lives.

It gave me time to think and gather my thoughts as to how long I was going to stay on Rhodes. It was at this point when it dawned on me once again that I was so lucky. I had experienced this feeling of freedom many times and I now realised what it tasted like... metaphorically speaking that is! I know I have said this before in a roundabout way, but I could go anywhere and do anything I wanted to do, within reason of course. I was able to do this without being an extension of anyone or anything. I was having an emotional moment, which for me was quite unusual, and still is. Was I slowly becoming addicted to this way of life? In all honesty, I think I probably was and I was totally in love with the concept. I was travelling around, spending my time exploring places and meeting people that I would not normally come across. I felt as if life's rich tapestry was reaching out to me and inviting me to look, feel and experience everything it had to offer. I suppose looking back I was unconsciously searching for the Holy Grail within me, which needed unlocking to get an insight to understand myself better. I hope that makes sense. I bet you thought I was going to make a reference to *Monty Python and the Holy Grail,* didn't you? Well, I didn't! But I have now! It's a brilliant film... it's great to watch. It's totally nuts and not everyone's ideal film, but it works for me!

It was great staying at the pensione with Katerina's family, but I couldn't stay too long. I have to admit that I felt very at ease there and I was getting quite comfortable. Maybe I was becoming too comfortable. As much as I liked it there, I also liked moving around. So, I made the conscious decision to make some enquiries about ferries to Piraeus in Greece.

I eventually made my way down the hill into a beautifully lit Lindos. I was aided by the moonlight and successfully avoided falling off the side of the hill and becoming an unpopular starter or main on some unsuspecting tourist's dinner table. I found a gyro stall and sat on a wall quietly devouring my little piece of tummy heaven, when I realised the time. It was around 8 o'clock. I wondered what time the last bus back to Rhodes Town was. It was quite unlike me to not find out these details in advance. As it turned out, I'd missed the last bus back. I was stuck in Lindos for the night and there was absolutely no way I was going to pay for a taxi back. I had three options. The first one was to find a cheap bed for the night, which I honestly didn't think was possible. The second one was to sleep on the beach or back up on the hill where I was earlier. The last one was to hitch a lift into Rhodes Town. It was basically a toss-up between hitching a lift or sleeping rough. I thought I'd try hitching first and I see how it panned out. If that fell flat on its face, then the trees with the bugs and animals on the hill would have the pleasure of my company for the evening. In the words of Baldrick in *Blackadder*, "I had a cunning plan".

I made my way to the main road leading out of Lindos. It wasn't particularly well lit at all. There were just a handful of faint lights dangling precariously, claiming asylum on the side of various telegraph poles. I stood under one of the lights so I could be partially seen and stuck my thumb out, hoping for the best. I didn't have a sniff of a lift for the first half an hour or so. Cars and lorries passed by without stopping. I don't blame them really. Who wants to pick up a dodgy looking bloke late at night? I know I would have thought twice about it myself. Then again, I once gave an involuntary lift to a well-dressed old man with a briefcase. I say involuntary because I didn't even know he existed until he opened the passenger door while I was sat daydreaming at a set of traffic lights. He opened the door to my little purple Renault 5 (it was a two-door hatchback) and placed himself next to me. He said, "Take me home". I actually remember thinking that he might have been suffering from dementia or something similar. Alternatively, he may have had an arsenal of weapons in his briefcase which I personally didn't want to get acquainted with! I asked him where he lived and he said, "I tell you when we get there". Great! Perfect! I was on my way to college and I was going to be late. In short, he gave me a shite load of directions, just like a twitching driving examiner. What I found quite amusing was the fact that he told me to stop, which I did, and he got out without a word and that was that. I wasn't even sure if he knew where he was going. I eventually arrived at college around an hour late. I gave my lecturer the reason for my lateness, and she raised her left eyebrow in typical Spock fashion. I don't think she believed me. I suppose it sounded like the age-old excuse of the dog eating my homework. Luckily, I wasn't given extra homework, detention or a hundred lines written in blood

So, we now return to Lindos. Just as luck would have it, a car eventually ground to a screeching halt with its inhabitants waving their knickers out of the windows like scarves at a football match and wolf whistling at the same time.

Anyway, I noticed three people inside. A man was driving with two women as passengers. They started speaking in Greek and said they were going to Rhodes Town. That was music to my ears. The gods were smiling on me. Or were they laughing at me? Probably the latter! Just as they were taking a risk giving me a lift, I was also taking a risk clambering into the back seat of the car. They didn't know me and I didn't know them. All was good, with no incidents except for my command of the Greek language, which they said was pretty crap. So we reverted to English which in a way I found a tad disappointing, but I saw the sense in it.

Isn't it funny how a fair amount of people can speak English? I suppose it's been one of the main international languages for a long time. It's taught in schools around the world. However, the British education system over the years has been quite slow on the uptake to teach children another language at an early age. I find that quite interesting. I suppose it's the fact that most countries compulsorily teach English as a second language, which has inadvertently not encouraged the Brits to learn another language. Some people have said and still say that because most people speak English, there is no need to learn another language. There are lots of differing views about this, ranging from an island mentality to colonisation and some even say arrogance. If you get a chance to read up about this, do it. It's actually quite interesting. However, these days, primary schools are now teaching primary school children French and Spanish as part of the curriculum.

Moving on, my rescuers were students. The driver and one of the girls were siblings and the other was a friend. The guy had borrowed his dad's car and they had spent the day in Lindos. After a good old chat with a few awkward moments here and there, we arrived in Rhodes Town unscathed. They dropped me off somewhere in the modern part of town. I thanked them in my best possible Greek and off I strolled once again into the night. You can't really get lost as you just head for the coast and meander towards the Old Town. I had a *Peaceful Easy Feeling* (to quote a well-known Eagles song). I eventually made it back to the pensione, totally shattered and went pretty much straight up to my free and very quiet, tranquil penthouse apartment. It was the envy of the whole of Rhodes!

The next day, after a great night's sleep and the morning chores, which were lovingly completed at breakneck speed, Katerina and I decided to go to Prasonisi beach. As I previously said, it's the place where the Mediterranean and the Aegean Seas meet. I had been intrigued by this natural phenomenon ever since Sophia had mentioned it. Katerina managed to acquire her mum's car for the day and we drove to the other end of the island. It was a good drive. We stopped for a coffee at a couple of tiny picturesque, roadside caravan type of establishments, with very questionable chairs and tables. I told Katerina about my short time in Lindos, which was accompanied by a couple of playful slaps. We also had quite a philosophical discussion about my evening's hillside thoughts.

All in all, the journey was around a couple of hours. We parked up on the hill away from the beach as we weren't really aware of the tide times and walked down. There were cars and camper vans already parked on the beach. Apparently, so we were told, it was safe to park on the beach but Katerina didn't want to risk it for obvious reasons. There was a little makeshift café set back, and a handful of refreshment vans serving drinks and food. Ahead of us was the island, which was accessible by foot once the tide had gone out. We could see the sea gradually creeping out so we sat in the café having a drink, chatting and taking in the view. To our right was the Aegean Sea and to our left was the Mediterranean Sea. I found the whole idea of a causeway to the island incredible and we could see it slowly unfolding in front of us. Katerina had seen it a few times and was a bit indifferent but she understood how I felt.

Once the tide had receded, we could see a wide, clear, wet and sandy path. We had a paddle in both seas, running from one sea to the other. We made it to the island, which accommodates a lighthouse. We obviously went to have a look at it. It looked like it needed a good coat of paint otherwise it was nothing out of the ordinary. We walked around the rest of the island for a couple of hours chatting for most of it, which was good. The island did have a few secluded bays with turquoise-coloured water which glimmered beautifully in the sun. It was very peaceful and far away from everything.

After we had exhausted this little peninsula which was currently physically connected to Rhodes, we walked back to the car. As it was still quite early-ish, we decided to drive to Lindos and visit one of Katerina's friends. Her friend ran a café/bar. Katerina said that Yianni would insist that we should have something to eat and he would not charge us. She had mentioned him before and that they went to school together. They had kept in touch ever since. I received another assortment of those laser-guided slaps when I asked her with all the subtleness I could muster, if he was husband material. After the barrage of slaps had subsided, she said with a knowing smile that I could vet him for her. Now this sounded intriguing. Would this be the man that would receive his share of slaps in a loving union? I was looking forward to this in a rather comical way.

We made it to Lindos, parked the car just outside the town and began to slowly stroll to Yianni's establishment. We walked past the shop where I was accused of shoplifting. Although it was only the day before, it seemed a long time ago. I'd mentioned the delightful episode to Katerina in the car early in the morning, and when I pointed out that we had just passed the shop, she wanted to go in. As we walked in, the owner recognised me and came to say hello. I introduced Katerina and they had a rather surprisingly pleasant conversational exchange. I say that because Katerina did possess huge elements of being a bit of an uncut diamond. In other words, rough around the edges! The conversation then spilled over into yesterday's antics. The owner looked embarrassed but Katerina put him at ease by saying that she would have done exactly the same. Charming! She laughed, looked me up and down, saying that I was actually OK for someone who didn't live on Rhodes and who spoke a dialect of Greek that no one understood. I suppose that was Katerina's way of getting the owner to accept me into the fold. Not that I needed to be accepted.

Having revisited the scene of the alleged crime which never took place, we made our way to Yianni's public institution and found him behind the bar chatting with a couple of guys. In typical Katerina fashion she shouted across the sparsely filled tables, "Yianni! Reh malaga!" If you haven't already done so, do feel free to look up the word 'malaga'. Of course, that was a head-turning moment, especially when Yianni came bounding from behind the bar and gave his school chum a huge hug. He was tall and slim and was sporting a closely cropped beard, which Katerina promptly rubbed and said something along the lines of "Get it off... NOW!" Katerina introduced us both, to which he replied in English, "Hmm, he's cute!" I then rather rapidly realised what Katerina meant by having him vetted. I don't think he was quite

Katerina's husband material. He sat with us, and ordered an assortment of food and some beers, which was great. We were then joined by a couple of Yanni's friends, who were equally non-husband material. When it came for us to leave, he insisted that it was all on the house, which was exactly what Katerina had said would happen. I wasn't going to argue with that. I mean, who in their right mind would? Seriously, though, it was very good of him to treat us.

On the way back, Katerina asked me what my plans were and how long I was going to stay. My immediate reply was along the lines of, "Are you trying to get rid of me because you want to move into my plush, fully furnished penthouse apartment?" I then asked her why she was asking. Her response to that was, "I've got used to you being around and I have a bit of a dilemma". She went on to say that I was the dilemma. You can decipher that last sentence for yourself. I'm not going anywhere near it! Some things are best left unexplained.

Anyway, she was hesitant at first but she eventually told me that she had an opportunity to study in America. She was both nervous and excited about it which was a perfectly understandable reaction. I told her that I was going to enquire about a ferry to

Piraeus, but I wasn't sure when I was moving on. I was reliant on the frequency of the ferries.

We spoke at length about Katerina's dilemma over the next couple of days. One of the many angles I was pushing was that she had to do what she wanted to do and not put her life on hold, waiting to see what other people's plans were. In other words, don't be reliant on what other people are doing. There's a whole world out there waiting to meet you. Having regrets about not doing things that you want to do is not helpful. If the opportunity is there and it feels right, then you should take it. To have the chance to travel and see more of the world is fantastic. It broadens your outlook on life and enriches you as a person. I was definitely encouraging her to go, but then again, I would do that, wouldn't I?

I eventually booked my ferry to Piraeus, which was leaving the following week. I had a very strange feeling as I was booking the ferry. I kind of felt sad as I was booking it. In saying that, I wasn't in much of a rush to leave but I felt I was getting too comfortable, so I needed a bit of a shake-up in more ways than one. In the meantime, I spent a lot of time pottering around with Katerina, which I really enjoyed.

One day, I was in the pensione with Katerina and Sophia, having a drink, when two South African girls who were staying came storming through the front door. One of the girls was crying quite uncontrollably, while the other was trying to unsuccessfully console her. It turned out that she had had her small day rucksack stolen, which contained among other things, her money, passport and not to mention a flight ticket to the Hague, where she was due to meet her mum. The poor girl was distraught. You have to remember that these were pre-mobile phone days. They were in their foetal stage. You could not just contact people that easily.

At that point, it made me think that it was all too easy to lose or have things stolen. I was always on high alert regarding things and situations around me and to this day, I still am. I never carried my passport, traveller's cheques or cash in my bag; well hardly ever. I had a very slim, skin-coloured type of wallet which I tied around my waist under my T-shirt. No one would know it was there, unless I was being fondled! Hmmm... now there's a jolly thought! At times, I would take it off as it got a little bit hot and sweaty. Having said that, the occasional wash was also required at times, as you could imagine! "What's he on about?" I hear you ask. "Is he talking about the cloth wallet or his body or both?" I'd say, use your imagination!

Anyway, to get another passport issued, the girl would have to go to the South African Embassy in Athens, which meant she would have to leave Rhodes and make her way to Athens. Luckily, she knew which hotel her mother was staying at in The Hague and managed to contact her to get her to help her out. It sounded very much like she was going to have to fly to Athens to sort out her passport. Her mum was able to pay for her flight and accommodation in Athens over the phone. Her friend was also a great help financially. What a predicament! With all this going on, I have to say that Sophia was brilliant. She allowed the girl to use her phone to contact her mother free of charge and supplied endless drinks, snacks and tissues. Sophia also managed to find the address of the South African Embassy in Athens along with the phone and fax number. Sophia encouraged the girl to phone the Embassy. The girl explained what had happened and then faxed a letter on Sophia's fax machine, explaining the exact same conversation in writing.

The night before I was due to leave for Piraeus, Katerina and I went out for a drink or two. We had a good night and I eventually staggered up the stairs to my penthouse suite for what was sadly to be the last time. I was already having pangs of regret about leaving but like I said earlier, I had to move on.

I dozed off pretty quickly. I suddenly woke to the sound of a loud muffled thud. I wasn't sure what it was or even where the noise was coming from. It took me a few seconds to realise that there was someone else entering my space. I reached for my torch, switched it on and scanned my little suite. I initially thought it was Katerina playing silly buggers like she normally did but much to my horror, lying on the floor near the stairs, was some lump of a bloke staring straight into the torch. As he was crawling towards me on all fours, I called out and asked him who the hell he was. There was no reply. He gradually came nearer and was within spitting distance. He leapt at me and put both his hands onto my cheeks (not my bum cheeks, I might add). He rubbed his lovely, thick cigarette-scented fingers all over my face. Mixed in with the added bonus of alcohol on his rancid breath he said, "Boolagi mou, Boolagi mou" which translated literally means, 'My bird, my bird'. In this case it probably meant, 'My love, my love'.

As you can probably imagine, I metaphorically shit myself! I momentarily froze like one would, as I was somewhat still in the clutches of the previous night's outing and in shock with this guy's smelly hands around my cheeks. I have to say that I was back in the real world almost immediately. I pulled his hands off my cheeks, and I looked around my luxurious abode. I was surrounded by odd bits of furniture comprising of dismembered chairs and tables in every nook and cranny. I literally jumped out of my sleeping bag in a semi-naked state, aided by the thought that this could all end up badly, especially for me! This bloke was bigger than me, as are most people. How he made it up those steep, dodgy, narrow stairs was beyond me. Anyway, the fact was he was there, and I was not happy. As a result of all this, I grabbed the nearest thing to me, which turned out to be a chair leg which was connected to the base of a seat. It was happily minding its own business, living out its last days communing with its other dismembered chair buddies. I eventually managed to pull the chair leg out complete with its seat. I swung the chair leg towards him and the seat flew off the end, just missing him and landed across the other side near the stairs with a massive bang. I have to say it was bloody loud! It woke some of the others as I could hear chattering going on downstairs. It was more in the way of, "What the fuck was that?"

I shouted out that there was an uninvited guest up here – well, words to that effect. As I was shouting, the man got to his feet and scrambled down the stairs. He tripped and he ended up at the bottom of the stairs. I then heard Sophia shouting in Greek. I leant over the banisters and witnessed Sophia administering a rather good and wholesome round of slapping sounds. I personally think the tried and tested frying pan method would have been better. You get a much better sound from it. To get an idea of what the hell I'm talking about, have a look at a *Bottom* clip with Ade Edmondson and the late great Rik Mayall. There's a clip from an episode called *Bottom Gas*. This particular scene from this episode is called *Gas Man Frying Pan Scene* and it can be found on YouTube. Have a look. It's over the top but it's hilarious.

It transpired that this man used to work at the Pensione a few years ago. He was now a policeman – the perfect role model for us all, don't you think? He obviously still had a copy of the key. Sophia promptly threw him out onto the street in no uncertain terms with the help of her husband and Katerina. She said that she would let his superiors know what had happened and demanded that she have the key back. Apparently, food had been going missing from the kitchen over a long period. This episode seemed to clear up the mystery, as Sophia thought it was her husband and Katerina having midnight nibbles. They both obviously denied it. They even took the matter to the European Court of Human Rights, which at the time was based in the local kebab restaurant. Katerina's dad also passed a cheeky comment saying that it explained the missing bottles of whisky and wine! As he said it, he looked at Katerina and my good self with one of those "I know it was you two" looks.. Katerina and I momentarily looked at each other. I quickly replied, saying that it probably accounted for the distillery smell on his breath. We suspected at that point that he knew we had been syphoning off a few bottles here and there. To be honest, he didn't seem that bothered.

The following morning, Katerina's dad changed the lock on the front and back door. I would have done the same regardless. The ferry wasn't leaving until mid-afternoon, so Katerina and I spent the morning walking and sitting around in a café, chatting. We were always chatting about something or other. I really enjoyed the chats we had. I was certainly going to miss all that. In the end, she had decided to go to America to study. She was going to work and get some money together and do a couple of weeks of 'safe and planned' travelling in America before her course started. I got the impression that her parents were apprehensive about it but they apparently had family out there which made it easier. The 'safe and planned' aspect was staying with relatives. Although Katerina was confident in her own environment, I could now see the vulnerability in her. In my humble opinion, it was good that she was shaking it up a bit.

After I had collected all my belongings and shoved them indiscriminately into my trusty travelling companion, I sat downstairs having a coffee and chatting with Katerina and her parents for the last time. The whole thing was tinged with a bit of sadness and excitement. The excitement part was about moving on. The sadness was obvious. I had quite enjoyed these social times with them. As we were saying our goodbyes, Sophia said in her own sweet way, that she would miss my miserable attempt at speaking the mother language. Katerina's dad gave me a small bottle of Metaxa brandy, saying that I would probably miss it now that I was leaving. I looked at Katerina with a 'We've been rumbled' look and we knew without any doubt whatsoever that he knew it was us.

After the customary hugs and kisses from Sophia and her husband, Katerina escorted me down to the port, where the ferry lay waiting to carry me off to a new experience. On the way down she said that her mum liked me and that she had asked Katerina lots of awkward questions. Katerina was like a politician... she could answer a question without actually answering it. She was very good at it! We gave each other an enormous hug and I thanked her for such a great time full of laughs, chats, drinks and of course... the slaps!

She practically pushed me into the arms of passport control. They ushered me through onto the boat after stamping my passport and the customary wave through. Once again, this was security at its best. After experiencing Israeli security, they are still the ones I wouldn't mess with. Great! Another stamp! Don't you just love passport stamps? Actually, I asked for the stamp. That was the last I saw of Katerina. She said she was not going to hang around for the boat to leave. I understood.

JOURNEY TO ATHENS

So, as usual on boats, as you know by now, I found and claimed my spot on the hard floor of deck class. Once again, my place of refuge was on the perimeter, the tried and trusted method. I placed my rucksack down and unrolled my sleeping bag as a statement to say this was my territory so bugger off! I looked around the deck and I have to admit that this part of the boat had definitely seen better days. There was rust bubbling through the white paintwork and the usual wafer-thin, green carpet was more or less non-existent. The toilets would be the main gauge of luxury, so as I needed a slash, I thought it might be an idea to pay a visit before the inevitable happened. It seemed like they must have been cleaned as there was a distinct smell of bleach hanging around. It was a pleasant experience for now. Let's see how long it would last for.

As I was walking back from the powder room, I noticed that someone had set up camp next to me. Initially, I wasn't sure about their gender as they were dressed in military fatigues from head to toe. As I got closer, I realised that it was an American guy.

How did I know that he was American? It was simple really. He had small American flags sewed onto the arms of his clothing and his rucksack was littered with them! If anyone had any anti-American leanings then he would have been great target practice. One thing I realised quite early on was that it was not a good idea to stand out. It's much better to blend in if you can. This guy stood out like a sore thumb.

Although he was wearing a military-style cap, I could make out he was quite fair. I sat down on my sleeping bag and we started talking. He seemed somewhat familiar in his fatigues. He took off his cap and I then realised that I had seen him in Jerusalem. You just could not miss him anywhere. When I first saw him, he was not in full military clothing apart from his trousers. His short, cropped blond hair and piercing blue eyes made him stand out like an active lighthouse. He was in the middle of Ben Yehuda Street with another guy with long, lanky hair, which probably housed a small number of socially acrobatic residents. They were both bent over a small portable stove, making what smelt like coffee, with people walking around them. I thought it was odd but didn't pay much attention to them as there was often a catalogue of strange people about. Jake, as he was known, spoke with a heavy southern American accent. I asked him if he'd been to Jerusalem and added that I thought I had seen him there. He weirdly asked me what he was doing when I saw him. So, I told him about the coffee, the stove and his nit-ridden friend. His reply was, "Yep, that was me!" Throughout this whole exchange, he showed no facial expression. Absolutely zilch!

It didn't take long for him to get onto the subject of politics, which is something I didn't want to discuss, especially with him. I was pretty sure we were poles apart in that respect. To say that he was right wing would have been an understatement. I would imagine that he would have most certainly been one of those people taking part on the assault on Washington's Capitol Hill and shouting his mouth off about the so called 'stolen election'. There would have been no doubt in my mind that he would have been in the thick of it. He was going on about all sorts of things, ranging from the United Nations (calling them United Nothings) to abortion, to gay rights and said that teachers were corrupters of children etc. As for anyone who had an ounce of left-wing political opinion, he referred to them as communists and 'Stalin's Hitmen'. The venom with which he said all this was quite funny but at the same time, it was quite scary. You really had to be there to witness what was coming out of his mouth. I couldn't believe my luck. I had been inadvertently landed with a complete psycho. So for my night-time activities, I was definitely going to sleep with one eye open, a whistle strapped to my hand while carefully spooning a well varnished baseball bat. What? Doesn't everyone have a baseball bat they call a friend?

Anyway, when everything was said and done, he made an awesome coffee. Mind you, he was not in the ferry steward's good books. His gas stove, his colourful language and his constant references to what a bunch of communists they were, didn't go down very well. The gas stove was definitely a safety issue, especially when the deck became a semi-sea of rucksacks! To be honest, the ferry wasn't particular busy. However, it didn't stop Jake making constant references to everyone being a commie. It was in complete contrast to the *Young Ones*, when Rick, Neil and Vyvyan called everyone and everything a fascist. If you haven't watched the *Young Ones* (not the Cliff Richard film, although I quite enjoyed watching the film) then I recommend that you do. It's complete chaos, but its pure genius, unlike Jake! You're never too sure what direction the episodes are heading in or even how they are going to end.

Initially, the evening went well. I read for quite a while as I hadn't really indulged myself very much when I was in Rhodes. Jake was conversing in his own sweet way with some people. I could hear his heavy southern accent mesmerising our fellow travellers so much that a few started to gradually drift away and jump overboard screaming with their fingers in their ears.

I momentarily looked up from my book and I noticed two guys who were standing by me looking over into the sea. I overheard them saying in their Aussie accents that, "The guy's a nutter. He's a complete fruit-cake!" These guy's comments about Jake made me laugh. At that point they turned around and apologised. They thought that we were travelling together. How could they think that? Did I look like I wanted to be verbally abused? If Jake's accent was grating on me enough, his overall outlook on life was just hell! I put them straight in no uncertain terms. I said that I wanted to move somewhere else but it would be rather obvious if I did. We all agreed that it would be social suicide. The idea of shutting up and biting the bullet was probably the more suitable option. We sat and chatted and shared what food we had. Katerina had made sure I had enough food and snacks for the journey. She was very caring really but she gave off an air of being a tough nut. I suppose it was a self-preservation thing for her. She was great fun, though.

After peering over the side of the ferry, watching the sun saying its goodbyes for the day, one of the Aussies pulled out a pack of cards. Not my favourite pastime, but it was OK. After a bit, we noticed the ferry was gently being pushed from side to side and that the wind was gradually making its way aboard like a stowaway. At this point, there were a few fellow travellers looking over the side with concern written all over their faces. This also included the C & G (Cabin and Gucci) brigade, who obviously felt the result of the wind winding its way through the open windows of the ferry, announcing its arrival. The C & G brigade arrived on deck and tentatively navigated their way around us, making sure they didn't brush up against us so that they wouldn't catch anything life threatening. They made their way to the back of the boat in order to survey the evening's commotion. I was already thinking that this was going to be a rough night with certain visions emerging in my head of Odysseus, making his way back from Troy to his home in Ithaca. If you haven't read this Ancient Greek piece of poetry by Homer, then you need to put it on your reading list... it's an epic!

It was getting late and it seemed that we were all ready to sleep through this potential storm. It was brewing nicely and boy, did it report itself for duty with its workmate... the rain. They made a great team. I was awoken by screams and sudden movements such as Jake rolling onto me. As I was completely immersed in my sleeping bag, I hadn't noticed the rain. In fact, I wasn't aware of anything outside my little den. I was completely out of it. Now that I was fully awake, as was Jake, I half expected him to say that we were being attacked by commies but even he wasn't that stupid. It was around half past one in the morning, when a couple of ferry staff from the on-board café started to direct us into the café space. They advised us to stay inside, as they were saying that there was a hefty storm coming our way. I have to admit that I was scared; actually, I was bloody terrified! I was on a tiny boat in a huge ocean. I'd never been on a boat in a storm. If the feeling was anything like bad turbulence on an aeroplane, then I'm sorry to say that I hadn't invested in an adult pair of pull-ups and a dummy.

How the boat made it through the storm was beyond me. At times the boat felt as if it was vertical. We were holding onto one of the many permanently static pieces of café furniture, like shit to a shovel. If you have any furry friends staying with you and you've lovingly cleaned out their litter tray, then you'll know what I mean. It was that bad! However, Jake made up for it at times with his constant moaning and verbal ablutions. Obviously, you couldn't mistake his deep southern American accent. That was the only amusing part of it. There were a couple of pools of sick over the lino floor, which trickled everywhere, making some rather interesting geometric patterns. It was accompanied with a stench that made you want to honk up. Luckily, it wasn't as visual as The Labyrinth's *Bog of Eternal Stench*. You couldn't get away from it. It was as if it had a mind of its own. We were being thrown around by the storm while at the same time, dodging the lively movement of someone's dinner. Lovely! I couldn't quite work out what was worse. The storm or finding myself covered in some poor soul's purged stomach!

This went on for around a couple of hours and it was a couple of hours of pure fear. I didn't know what was going to happen. None of us did. The bar/café staff had buggered off and had left us to our own devices; not that we had many choices. The only choice us deck people really had was to sit tight and hope for the best. The whole situation was out of everyone's hands. A few of us managed to park our bums onto the seats as the storm started to subside and miraculously, just like a magician pulling rabbits out of some knackered, moth-eaten top hat, the bar staff returned. They surveyed and sniffed the air in the café, opened the windows and doors. They made some joke about the state of the place (or maybe it was about us, who knows) and started to mop up and disinfect the floor. The look of disgust on their faces as they were cleaning was great. To be honest, I don't blame them. Would I want to clean up someone else's projectiles? Nope! Unfortunately, I didn't think about taking a picture of the episode at the time, but I suppose the events and trying to survive in some capacity had taken precedent. It was definitely worthy of a photo, though!

The staff ushered us out onto the deck while they finished cleaning up. They said we could come back once they had finished. We all appreciated their offer as the deck, which would have been our nightly slumber, was drenched. Personally, I couldn't wait to get out into the fresh night air, as the café was rather smelly, which you would expect. The smell of vomit and bleach was overpowering. By this point, the sea was much calmer and the air was fresher, if that makes any sense. The contrast to the earlier phenomenon was amazing. It was as if nothing had happened. No beating rain, no vocalised wind; absolutely nothing.

After I exchanged various comments, experiences and feelings with the others, including those who were still visibly suffering, we were let back into the café. Some mentioned that their rucksacks had been attacked and infiltrated with vomit. I was very lucky. I don't know how it happened and I'm certainly not complaining, but mine was vomit free. I don't think I would have been able to cope otherwise.

The staff made us tea and coffee free of charge, which was a nice touch. To cover themselves they asked us to keep it quiet. Someone asked them how they were going to get around it. They replied by saying that they would say that some of their stock of tea and coffee was ruined due to the storm. One of the cafe staff commented that at least we were all still alive. Never was a truer word spoken!

I suppose they felt sorry for us. In fact, I felt sorry for all of us and that included the designer label brigade. It was a bloody horrible experience. We were at the complete mercy of nature. I caught up with Jake and for the first time since I met him, he was muted. He didn't have much to say. He really didn't have to say anything... his face did the talking. Although I found him irritating and embarrassing at times, I actually felt sorry for him. I wouldn't wish what we went through on anyone. Most of us thought that we were finished; that we were fish food. It's amazing what goes through your mind in a matter of seconds in those situations. My mum and brother featured quite prominently. I've heard about people saying, "My life flashed before my eyes", and I couldn't really understand it. However, I now totally understood.

The next few hours passed peacefully and Rosy's fingers started to push their way onto the horizon, marking the start of a new day and there was not a hint of bad weather. The whole thing was a bit like an awful dream, as if it had never really happened. But it did happen and unfortunately, it was a very frightening natural event. It's a strange thing to say, but I'm glad I experienced it even though it was complete hell at the time. In hindsight, I'm even happier that I came out the other end alive!

Anyway, let's get back to more earthy matters. I needed to pay a visit to the powder room, fearing the worst from Poseidon's earlier antics, and found to my amazement that it was spotless. Well, not exactly spotless, but in a better state than you would expect. Yes, someone had been busy cleaning! It still had that lingering incontinent smell mixed in with a heavy dose of bleach. To be honest, at the time I was trying to decide which of the two was the most rank... the smell of the bleach or the incontinent bouquet. I clearly didn't have enough to do! The intoxicating whiff seemed to hang around in the toilet longer than it did in the café area. In saying that, after a few hours and much use, the toilet resembled the café floor during the storm. Some things never change!

A couple of C & G passengers came down to see how we were. I thought that it was a decent and caring thing to do. They looked very well-to-do. They were very well off... in the money. They had a genuine look of concern plastered across their faces. We were asked how we felt, what we did and whether we were allowed to shelter inside. There were lots of questions. They seemed truly interested. It wasn't just lip service. They were also sharing their feelings about the storm, wondering if they were going to survive. They were terrified as well. I would say that everyone on the ferry would have had the same emotions, with the exception of a few adrenaline junkies. I suppose we are all the same really. Just before they left, they went to the bar and asked the staff to prepare large flasks of tea and coffee for us poor beggars along with some packaged croissants and pastries, which they paid for. None of us expected that! Such lovely people! It went a little way to confirming that there are some good people in this world who acknowledge people regardless of what they look like.

ATHENS

We eventually rolled into Piraeus around mid-morning and the first thing that struck me was how big the port was. I looked at the port from the deck and it didn't seem that particularly busy. It all seemed quite quiet and grey; as if it was shrouded in its own little world. There were a couple of ships, a few lorries, vans, cars and a handful people going about their daily jobs. I actually thought that it would be a lot busier than it was. I have to admit, I was a little bit spooked by it all. It was probably nothing but the place felt as if there was an air of the past entering the present. It was weird.

As always when entering a new environment, I had to find somewhere to stay. I strolled through security. No one paid any attention to me. I suppose it's all changed now given certain world events, but it still amazed me how lax security was back then. I decided to stay in the Piraeus area for now as I thought it would be a lot cheaper compared to the centre of Athens. I was also aware that there was a good metro service into the centre of Athens. Everyone else seemed to be heading into Athens.

I had arranged to meet a small group of people in Syntagma Square that evening around 6pm. It was in the centre of Athens. As for Jake, I didn't see him get off the ferry. Maybe he had been tied up and handcuffed to the toilet cistern. Better still, maybe he had been keelhauled by the staff and conveniently forgotten about. He obviously did get off because our paths crossed again in Thessaloniki in Northern Greece. I'll tell you about that later when I eventually get there, but for now I have the lovely sights of Piraeus to explore.

As I said earlier, I would have to find a place to lay my weary head. It had been a long, emotional night. Armed with my vomit-free rucksack on my back and my ammunitions bag around my sweaty and salty neck, I picked a street and wandered up it. I noticed that there were a few cheap, grubby-looking hotels, hostels and pensiones. I popped into a few asking about prices and availability of rooms and beds as some of them were dormitories. The cheap ones were fully booked as you would expect. I decided to carry on walking away from the port, where in theory it would be cheaper (not always the case) and availability would be better. Don't forget, as I have said before, these were pre-mobile phone days. If I'd had a mobile phone, it would have been far easier to find somewhere to stay. Mind you, thinking about it, even now I much prefer travelling without one. It's one less thing to lose and the thought of not being connected to the outside world appeals to me.

Anyway, just by chance I found a small and cheap hostel which was a good walk from the port. It was on the second floor above a general food shop, which was handy. If you blinked you would miss the sign. From the outside, the building itself was tatty and run-down. However, once I went up the stairs and into the hostel, I was pleasantly surprised. I asked about a room and I was shown to a small room. It was a good price. The room was basic but pretty much spotless with the odd dent and cigarette burn. Otherwise, it was fine. The shared toilet and shower were also very clean indeed. There were unlimited tea and coffee facilities with a basic breakfast of croissants, pastries and toast. Some of the croissants and pastries were a little bit on the stale side, but hey, that was fine. I had inherited stale croissants before in Jerusalem with Susy. There are worse things out there. I'm not one to argue about things like that. The hostel reminded me of the pension in Rhodes but without the brilliant hosting of Katerina and family. However, this place was no way as cheap as my previous penthouse accommodation. That certainly was a one-off!

I paid for a couple of nights, went up my room, lay on the bed without even looking at the view from my window and that was it for a couple of hours. When I woke, I momentarily wondered where the hell I was. I didn't immediately recognise my surroundings. It was a strange feeling but I quickly realised where I was. I crawled rather slowly out of what seemed like a deep sleep and was hoisted back into the real world. I had a shower in lukewarm water and decided to make my way into the centre of Athens. I was given a free tourist map (I'll take anything that's free) and was directed to a bus stop by the owner of the hostel. I suppose I could have used the Metro, but the bus was definitely the better option. I was able to see more of the city above ground and it was cheaper. I was told that this bus passed Syntagma Square and went near to the Acropolis. It was certainly a great place to start, especially as I was going to meet the others later.

After being on the bus for a while, I was beginning to nod off again as the bus rolled around the streets. I decided to listen to The Boss (Bruce) to stop me dozing off. In between the buildings, I eventually caught glimpses of the Acropolis and the Parthenon, hovering high up in the distance. It was as if we were playing peek-a-boo... now you see me, now you don't. Perched on top of a hill, it looked very grand and seemed to have an air of aloofness. It was making it own a statement of its importance. I would imagine that was the whole idea back in the days of the Ancient Greeks. The Acropolis was dedicated to the goddess Athena to thank her for the Athenians' military success over the Persian Empire. The Acropolis and the Parthenon (the temple) were also symbolic. They were to show the known world of the time the dominance and power of Athens.

I'd asked the bus driver to let me know when we had arrived at Syntagma Square and he was kind enough to do so. I thanked the driver in my best Greek and literally jumped off the bus before he could say, "Re malaga, your Greek is rubbish!" My immediate thought was how busy Syntagma Square was. There were cars, vans and buses everywhere and the noise was just incredible. I took my life into my hands and tried to cross the road to get onto the Square. It was like playing a game of chicken. I suppose I could have used a conventional crossing, but this was much more fun... and dangerous! I have to say, the Greeks certainly liked using their horns and hanging out of their vehicle's windows, conversing with their hands and loud voices. There were some pretty good hand gestures and very colourful, in the heat of the moment, language. Anyway, I successfully navigated my way across the road. Syntagma Square is literally a square with traffic around it; a bit like how Trafalgar Square used to be. As I looked around the square, I noticed a fountain and I assumed that this would be the best place to meet everyone later, as we hadn't exactly said where we would meet on the square. I hoped that the others would be tapping into my logic.

Syntagma Square is also known as Constitution Square. Historically, it is said that this is where the Athenians rose up against King Otto of Greece to demand a constitution in 1843. Overlooking the square, is the Royal Palace of King Otto, who incidentally was the first King of Greece. However, nowadays it is used as the Hellenic Parliament.

I quickly had a wander around the square and noticed the Hellenic Parliament across the road. I didn't know what it was at the time, until I tagged along onto a tourist group with a guide. It was rather naughty I know, but it was very informative. The guide, who had the embarrassing and obligatory multi-coloured umbrella held high, spoke about the Hellenic Parliament, King Otto and the Constitution. He pointed out that in front of the Parliament building was the Tomb of the Unknown Soldier. The guide then began to cross the road, waving his umbrella at a crossing and like a flock of sheep, everyone followed.

The tomb was guarded by two Presidential Guards, who were dressed in the traditional military dress code of the time. These soldiers are known as

'Evzones'. They are normally dressed in a white tunic, white tights and shoes that had what look like small pompoms on the end of them. They were also wearing waistcoats and red berets with long tassels. With all this said, they were both holding a rifle which I imagine was loaded. I don't think my description is doing them any visual justice so when you get a minute Google them. In a strange way, they looked like a cross between Tommy Cooper and a ballet dancer, which doesn't bear thinking about. So, I followed suit and had quick nose around the tomb.

Going back to the pompoms, I thought at the time that they were a strange addition to an already weird costume. However, the guide told his tourist congregation that the pompoms actually had a use. Traditionally, small knives were hidden within them for kicking the enemy. It was a very effective weapon during close combat. That actually reminded me of a James Bond film (*From Russia with Love*) where a female SMERCH / SPECTRE operative had a pair of dagger shoes with retractable poison-tipped blades which was similar to a flick knife.

Once I'd finished looking around, I spoke to a couple of people, like I normally do, from the congregation of sheep. I made my way through the National Garden and spent some time wandering, which was beautiful, especially the trees. I love trees! I sat under a tree, pulled out my book from my bag and had a good read. It was good to be away from the noise and urgency of the square. However, the dulcet tones of the car horns were ever present. From the National Garden, I walked to the main road and crossed into an area that seemed to have a lot of hustle and bustle. There were lots of tourists with cameras and bags draped over their shoulders. This was a pickpocket's paradise! Tourists were milling around looking at café and restaurant prices and trying to decide which one of the five million establishments to graze in. Standing outside the restaurant were waiters trying to entice people in. Before they could even answer, they would be seated, taped to a table with a napkin around their necks and a menu thrust under their noses. This is obviously an exaggeration but you can envisage how it looked. I have to say, I found it massively entertaining!

As always, I didn't have a Scooby Doo as to where I was going but I carried on walking through the pretty, narrow side streets littered with souvenir shops and cafés. After a few minutes and with the smell of cooked food entertaining the afternoon air, I eventually stumbled across what I thought was the base of the Acropolis, which was at the end of one of the streets. I was now quite excited. I remember as a child learning about the Ancient Greeks and Romans. The buildings intrigued me. I have always been in awe of the construction of all ancient buildings and how they have survived for so long. This interest stayed with me and led me to study Classical History and associated literature at university some time later.

I was now at the base of the hill on which the Acropolis was built. However, scaffolding had been erected around it. Unfortunately, it wasn't long before it was time for the Acropolis to close for the day. I decided to go back another day (probably with everyone else) so I could spend the whole day nosing around the area. I had a quick walk along one side of the base and came across an amphitheatre down the hill. I was quite excited at the prospect of going back. In fact I was very excited!

Anyway, it was around 5 ish and I decided to head back towards Syntagma Square to meet the others. Hopefully they'd turn up. You could never tell what was going to happen. Sometimes people turned up and at other times they didn't. I made my way back through the National Garden, and wandered casually towards my destination – to the fountain in the middle of the square. Hopefully, they would have the same idea about the fountain as I did. When I arrived a little before six, they were already sitting on the circular wall of the fountain. Great minds and all that!

In total, there were now seven of us. It was originally five but two girls had tagged along from the International Youth Hostel (IYH). They were all saying that their hostel was overpriced. I mentioned my experience of two IYHs which were definitely pricey. That was with regard to the facilities and also sleeping in a dormitory for the price. That's one reason why I didn't go with them. I told them about my temporary humble abode, which was not too far from the port. I said that it was actually pretty good and relatively cheap and I had a room to myself. I mentioned that it was a bit of a distance from the centre though. That was the only drawback really. The IYH was more central but in the scheme of things, my hostel's location wasn't a problem. I had all the time in the world.

We wandered around the immediate area and ended up in the Plaka district, which was very near to the Acropolis. The Acropolis was majestically lit up, portraying itself in its former glory. We sat chatting and eating next to some kind of memorial. It had wooden bench seats that felt like you were sitting on a hormonal porcupine... not that I have ever sat on one! Speaking of which, Echo and the Bunnymen recorded an album called *Porcupine*, which I love.

They're not everyone's cup of tea, but for me, they were brilliant. Going back to the wooden bench seats, I think we were lucky not to have shared any splinters between us.

It was a pleasant evening; very chilled. Everyone seemed to get on and there were no larger-than-life personalities, which was good. The two Aussies (who I'd met on the ferry) were good company and very funny. They didn't have a care in the world. Within the group there was a German couple who spoke pretty good English compared to my limited German. The new recruits (two girls) were French and they were from Strasbourg. Again, their English was very good as opposed to my French. I've said this earlier and I feel I have to mention it again, but in terms of learning languages, the Europeans certainly put us to shame. I suppose the argument that I keep hearing is that English is the main international language and because of that, we don't bother.

The following morning and after a good breakfast, we all met up again at the fountain on Syntagma Square to go up to the Acropolis. My humble abode offered me a selection of very stale, pre-1989 Tarom Airlines-style pastries and croissants. They were going to throw them away, so I took them and shared them out with everyone. I pointed out that they were old but edible.

Anyway, as I had mentioned the night before, the Acropolis site was quite big and I was excited about having a look around. We walked through the National Garden and stumbled across what we could only describe as ruins of some kind. We didn't know what the site was until we left and saw a sign in Greek and English which told us that it was the Temple of Olympian Zeus. To be honest, none of us were any the wiser.

Back in the day, around 5th Century BC when the Acropolis and the Parthenon were built, I would guess that the surrounding community was sprawled out like it was today. The only difference would be that the Acropolis was obviously not a historical landmark (as it is today) but was part of a very active and thriving, working Athenian community. It had a whole manner of temples, formal buildings and shops littered near to its base or within its vicinity.

We made our way onto a partial gravel path with what looked like unsecured scaffolding hovering all around us, which I personally thought was a bit dodgy. No one else seemed to bat an eyelid. Who knows what the mischievous Zeus and Company would drop from the heavens, just for their entertainment? The Company bit that I'm referring to were the modern day Athenian contingent working on repairing whatever they were repairing, if that makes any sense! Still... I suppose it made it exciting!

The path, which was on a gradient, took us along one side of the perimeter away from the amphitheatres. We entered the Acropolis and we all noticed how big the site was and how high we were. We could see the whole of Athens. How on earth did they get all the materials onto this hill? It's an amazing piece of engineering, as were all the classical buildings around at that time, including the Ancient Egyptians' structures etc. They have all certainly stood the test of time.

The Acropolis has been standing for about two and a half thousand years and has withstood devastating damage and change over the years. The Persians attacked Athens in 480 BC, when they burned and looted the Old Parthenon. To prevent further pillaging, the Athenians managed to bury their remaining sculptures inside the surrounding natural caves, which I found to be quite interesting. After Rome converted to Christianity in 6th Century AD, a number of the buildings on the Acropolis became Christian churches, most notably, the Parthenon, which was dedicated to the Virgin Mary, and the Erechtheion, which became a chapel. The goddess Athena would have been turning in her grave, if she had one that is! In 1687, an Ottoman ammunition dump, which was situated inside the Parthenon, was blown up during a Venetian siege. This assault damaged the Parthenon quite substantially. Over time many priceless artefacts were stolen, vandalised or destroyed.

After the Greek War of Independence against the Ottomans in 1822, the Acropolis was given back to the Greeks in a state of ruin. During the Ottoman period, the British acquired certain artefacts from the Acropolis. The Greek government strongly disapprove of the fact that the British still possess their artefacts and feel that the sculptures should be returned to their rightful place. I totally agree with that view. They should be returned to their place of origin.

In a nutshell, this is what happened. In 1801, Thomas Bruce, the Earl of Elgin, began to remove the Parthenon's sculptures. This was done with the so-called permission of the occupying Ottoman forces. It has been disputed that permission had been gained to remove the sculptures. Half of the Parthenon's sculptures were removed and were sold to British Museum. They are presently still in the British Museum today, where they are known as the Elgin marbles.

In 2021, it was recommended by UNESCO that the British Museum should reopen a dialogue with Greece regarding their stance on returning the sculptures. UNESCO's recommendation was bluntly refused by the British Museum. I would think that if these sculptures were returned to Greece, it would open the floodgates for the return of other artefacts taken from other countries. If this were to happen, I would also go as far to say that other countries who had taken artefacts would experience pressure to return them to their rightful owners.

During World War 2, it is said that approximately thirty-two mortar bombs exploded in and around the Acropolis area, causing a surprisingly small amount of damage. However, in saying that, the Parthenon sustained two direct hits but it is still in one piece to tell the tale. Given that these structures are so old, I still find it amazing they are still standing after sustaining so much trauma.

We spent most of the day looking around the Acropolis and sitting on various rocks, taking in the view of Athens. There were two things we noticed while we were looking out over Athens. First, we saw another hill in the distance with a building on the top of it. The second thing we saw was the infamous cloud of smog. This toxic cloud was literally just floating there doing nothing. Athens' air quality these days is what is termed as moderate. For years, the air pollution in Athens had become a huge issue. It had become a priority. Apparently, it was awful, especially in the height of the summer, which resulted in breathing issues for some people.

I had heard of a certain plan of action that the Athenians had put into place regarding this. They were generally encouraged to either use public transport, or share their vehicles with neighbours and friends. The way that it worked was like this. It operated on a vehicle odd and even number plate system. For example, if a registration plate was an even number, then you were allowed to drive that vehicle for the day. On the next day, it would be odd numbers. It basically went on like this. The number plates would alternate every other day. It was designed to cut down the pollution by having fewer vehicles on the road and people could help each other.

However Greeks being Greeks, definitely had other ideas. They had various number plates made up. These false number plates would correspond with the different days and they would swap them over when they needed to. I suppose they had to make sure that they didn't have an accident or jump lights, especially with the police lurking. I'm sure some were caught. I might add that all this was hearsay.

We had finished looking around the Acropolis, so we pottered around the base of the hill looking at the amphitheatres and gave a very brief, and very rubbish rendition of Hamlet's 'To be or not to be'. We took a short stroll to Philopappos Hill, and took a look at Socrates' so-called prison. He was imprisoned for "corrupting the youth" by publically supporting the rival city-state of Sparta and questioned the established conceptions of justice and morality. We then moved on to get a drink, a bite to eat and sat chatting again.

This particular group of people that I had been with the past couple of days were quite talkative. There was a lot of laughing, some deep conversations and teasing, which made the whole time that we'd been together a good experience. I have to say that it's not often it happens when complete strangers get together. The unusual thing for me was that we all exchanged addresses so early on. It just showed you how relaxed we were with each other. I never really gave my address out. I only ever did if I felt very comfortable with whoever I was with, otherwise it was a no-no. In saying that, at times, I did give out false addresses especially if someone was being pushy. They would end up somewhere in Streatham in South London.

We loosely planned what we would do over the next few days. There were free museums that we could visit, parks to chill out in, markets to rummage through and of course my favourite pastime... pottering! We spent a lot of time together but for a couple of days we did our own thing. We all agreed that it was important to have our own space. However, we would often meet at our usual location (Syntagma Square) in the evening and go on from there. My thing, as you well know by now, was to wander through the streets. I loved doing that. It gave me time to think.

On one of my particularly wet pottering days, I ended up walking up Mount Lycabettus, which was the hill opposite the Acropolis. I could have taken the funicular railway but, as usual, I didn't want to spend the money. The higher I climbed, the better the views became. Perched on top of this wooded hill was the church of Agios Georgios (St. George). Once at the top, I decided to go into the church and just sit. The outside of the building itself was painted white, while the inside of the church was your typical Greek Orthodox arrangement. I have to say it was very peaceful. All the outside noise seemed non-existent. I pottered around the site a bit more and sat looking over the whole of Athens, as far as the sea. Opposite, I could also see the Acropolis seated majestically on top of the world, for all to see. That would have been a definite statement of power in its day. It was truly magnificent, even on a rainy day like this!

Talking of rain, my boating shoes were letting in rain and the odd small pebble, which wasn't great. They squelched with every step I took. I had the distinct feeling that they were begging me to put them out of their misery. To be honest, they were pretty hammered so they needed to be put to rest.

With that decided, I started looking for some inexpensive but suitable pieces of fabric to put my feet in. I was walking around for a while, all the time looking out for something dirt cheap. I'd seen a couple of pairs but they were too pricey. I was walking towards the Acropolis, when I stumbled across a flea market. They sold everything. It was mostly used and vintage stuff. I had a good nose around and eventually came across a stall that sold ex-army clothes and boots. They were reasonably priced and with a bit of haggling here and there, I was sure that I would find something. I rummaged through a large box of dusty old army boots and eventually came across a pair in my size. They were shin length, brown leather with a warm lining. With a bit of haggling, I only ended up paying around £3.50 sterling which, in my opinion, was a bargain. They were perfect! After drying my feet off with my hands, the guy who owned the stall must have felt sorry for me because he threw in a thick pair of used socks. To be fair, they looked as if they had never been worn. In return, he said that I could buy him coffee. Seemed fair enough to me!

While sipping our drinks, we chatted in a mixture of English and my painfully bad Greek. He told me that he ran the stall to fund his history studies at university. He was a genuinely nice guy.

 I wasn't going to meet up with the rest of the guys until the following day, so I decided to go back to my room to rest, listen to some music and have a read. I lovingly fondled my newly acquired, ex-army issue boots, spoke to them tenderly about breaking them in and generally chilled out for the evening. As I was writing this, my mind wandered over to the Woody Allen film *Everything You Always Wanted To Know About Sex *But Were Too Afraid To Ask* starring Gene Wilder, who falls in love with a sheep. Such a brilliant film! Obviously, I didn't fall in love with a sheep, but instead, I fell in love with my boots. However much I loved my boots, they didn't look as good in lingerie as Daisy the sheep. The film is hilarious. If you have any time, you need to watch it.

ATHENS TO THESSALONIKI

An interesting 36 hours after leaving Athens

Over the next few days, we just pottered around together. Eventually, we all decided to go to Thessaloniki, on the northern coast of Greece. The two French girls and German couple decided to get the train, which in hindsight was probably the better and safer option! The two Aussies and my good-self decided to hitch a ride. We all decided to meet up at the IYH in Thessaloniki over the next couple of days, depending on how us hitchers got on.

That morning, I met up with everyone at their hostel. The two groups went their separate ways. One group went to the main train station and the other group (us) ended up at a lorry drivers' cafe on the toll road. The Aussies were told about this by one of the travellers at the hostel. He said that it would be easier to get a lift there as opposed to the roadside. It made total sense, so that's what we did. Initially, we tried to get a lift together but that wasn't working out so we all split up. That worked like a dream. We all got lifts quite quickly.

The guy who offered me a lift had more or less just arrived. As he was climbing out of the cab of his lorry, I pounced and asked him if he was going to Thessaloniki. In fact, I didn't even string a sentence together. I just said, "Thessaloniki?" He nodded and we both gave the thumbs-up sign simultaneously. Result! He pointed to the cafe and inferred that I go with him. I agreed as I was peckish.

He was tall and lanky with long, black, greasy hair and a handlebar moustache that any WW1 army officer would be proud of. He was a man of few words... in fact he didn't speak much at all. I tried to make conversation but didn't get much back. I was beginning to wonder if this journey with this particular guy was a good idea. I was definitely beginning to have second thoughts. Should I look for someone else? In the end, I stuck with it. I have to say that this was not one of my better decisions. I should have gone with my gut feeling; but hey, you live and learn and I'm here to tell the tale!

Anyway, we were at the café for around an hour making smaller than minuscule small talk. Looking around, it was most definitely, a 'real man's' café. The air was littered with was lots of testosterone, shouting out the word 'malaka' and lots of banging on tables. It was quite funny really. It wasn't really much of a step up from our Neanderthal ancestors.

I had a sandwich and the guy, who was called Dimitri (I got that much out of him), had quite a large fry-up, which was washed down with a couple of beers. He ordered me a couple of large Stella Artois beers, which, quite frankly, was not a good idea! It was around midday when we finished. He paid for it all. That was very good of him.

Unfortunately, I got pretty hammered. As I mentioned earlier, I've never been a great drinker. The lorry cab seemed high and I haphazardly climbed into the cab, without the help of a mountain harness. I vaguely remember pushing my rucksack into the cab. How I actually managed to get it up there was beyond me! I was just thankful that I'd got it in. Once he got behind the steering wheel, we set off. I not only realised that I had been drinking and was a tad out of my box, but he had also been drinking and he was bloody driving! This was not a good start by a long shot. I asked him if he was OK to drive. He said that he was fine by giving me the thumbs-up. He understood that much, which got me thinking that he understood more than he let on.

As you've probably already worked out, I'm a lightweight in terms of alcohol but to be fair to him, he actually seemed alright. In saying that, my judgement at the time had to be questioned! He put some music on and he started singing and he surprisingly asked me some questions about myself in Greek and I returned the compliment by asking him a couple of questions in a mixture of Greek and English. It was a pleasant exchange and I began to think that he wasn't too bad. As time went on, the motion of the lorry and the 'Stella' were beginning to make it difficult for me to keep my eyes open. He obviously noticed because he asked me if I wanted to have a kip in the back of the cab. I was so tired I foolishly agreed. I climbed onto the surface of the bed in the back of the cab, clutching my munitions bag. I also made sure my money belt was secure around my waist.

I put my head down and that was it; I was in dreamland. In fact, when I woke up, there was no light. It was dark and it seemed that we had stopped. I heard the door slam and the door being locked from what I assumed was the outside. I had absolutely no idea what was going on, where I was or where he had buggered off to. To this very day I still don't know why he got out. Anyhow, I woke up very thirsty. I took my torch out and searched around the cab for some water. Just by chance, I came across a large bottle of coke or what I thought was coke. Obviously, not the white powdery stuff! I was desperate for a drink so I started to unscrew the lid. I found the bottle unusually slippery but thought nothing of it. I put the bottle to my lips and began the process of taking a swig. I noticed that the consistency of the coke was somewhat less fluid than normal. As I put the bottle to my lips, the liquid entered my mouth. I realised that it wasn't coke. I then came to the rapid conclusion that it was probably engine oil. It was an easy mistake, given that it was so dark and that coke was the same colour as engine oil. The fact was, I was 'as dry as a nuns' and desperate for a drink, so to be honest, I wasn't really thinking straight. You're probably thinking that I wasn't thinking straight anyway. And you would be right! Who in their right mind would be in the middle of nowhere, locked in a lorry and drinking engine oil? Who knew what was going to happen next!

Once I realised what was in the bottle, I spat it out behind the passenger seat like there was no tomorrow and started wiping my mouth with a smelly old cloth that was lying around. I didn't know which was worse, the rancid cloth or the engine oil. All the while, I was continually spitting out the oil. Luckily, I didn't swallow any but I could taste it along with the smell of the cloth. For all I knew, the cloth could have been a pair of his underpants. I couldn't really see what it was. What a wonderful thought! The combination of the oil and the cloth was bloody horrible! I wouldn't recommend ordering that coalition in a café!

As I eventually got rid of any lingering leftover tastes, I heard the key being put into the lock of the door. At that point, I quickly swung my feet back around and lay down pretending to still be asleep. I heard him climb in, start the lorry and begin to drive off. A few thoughts started to go through my head once again such as, how on earth did I end up worse for wear, in the back of a lorry being driven to Thessaloniki by some bloke with a moustache that could simultaneously touch the insides of both lorry doors!

After a little while, I pretended to wake up. At this point, my throat was absolutely bone-dry so I asked Dimitri if he had any water. To my amazement he gave me a small, sealed bottle. Water had never tasted so good! After a few minutes, he pulled over into what I can only assume was a lay-by. What now? I was more than beginning to get a little bit nervous but I don't think I showed it. He turned around to me and said, "Nicc... I sleep! Ich Schlaffen!" He also said it in Greek. I have absolutely no idea why he had to say it in three languages.

I replied by saying, "That's fine, it's no problem. I'll get out from the back and sit on the seat and you can get in and sleep."

I said all this with animated hand signals so that there would be clear water between what I was saying and potentially what he wanted! A perfectly natural answer to his request to sleep... or so I thought.

So, as I said, it was a perfectly natural and normal request from Dimitri and I gave a perfectly normal response. The man was tired and he had probably completed his quota of kilometres for the day, if that law applied in Greece. To be honest, I wasn't sure, but I gave him the benefit of the doubt.

To my horror, he answered me by saying that it was OK for me to stay where I was and that he would get in next to me. Can you picture what was going through my head? Major alarm bells the size of a cow started ringing at this point! Now imagine you're at a tennis tournament watching a game with a pretty good rally going on. That's what it was like with a dialogue of... No! Stay! I will get in! No, I'll get out! NO! YES! NO!! YES!! NOOO!!! YESSSS!!! JUICE!! Not bloody likely if I've got anything to do with it! This went on for what seemed like a time and eternity. Looking back, the whole episode reminded me of some kind of lorry driver's mating ritual, which I certainly did not want be party to. In the end, I very, very, very reluctantly gave in but I was on very high alert. I actually remember thinking what the fuck was I doing?

Now I don't know if you've ever been in the back of a lorry cab (and why would you, unless...) but you would really struggle to fit two people in. It's that narrow. He began to clamber into the space, which was layered with just a thin smelly mattress with an equally smelly cover. I'd never really noticed it earlier but certainly noticed it now. I was definitely beginning to panic at this point, and once again, I tried not to show it.

I decided to lie on my side with my arse up against the back wall of the cab, propping my head up on my hand and looking over him. Thinking about it, whichever position I lay in would have been a no-win situation. It turned out that he initially lay on his side with his back to me and the rear cab wall. He began to shuffle around, which made me feel quite uncomfortable. How was I going to get out of this? God only knows! As I lay there, fully awake, I could smell what I assumed was his body odour rising past my already abused nostrils and on its way to the roof of the cab. This was where it would linger like an unwelcome guest, demonically laughing and shouting out "You've had it mate!"

He lay there motionless for a while, which was good. I actually thought he was asleep at this point. I was emotionally and physically drained by now and I started to nod off once more. I had to make sure that

I stayed wide awake one way or the other. My body must have jolted realising that I was falling asleep and Dimitri had sensed some movement. In that moment, he started moving his arm and scratched his head, then his chest and then his thigh. His arm just lay on the top of his thigh for a minute or two. It could have even been thirty seconds. I don't really know. It was difficult to put an estimation of time on all this, especially with my mind racing as it was!

I was now beginning to get agitated and was thinking of taking my chances out on the motorway. As I was thinking this, his arm was on the move once more, just like a prowling lion going after a slippery eel. He started scratching his back and slowly moved down to his bum. This is where I lost sight of his hand. I could see his arm but not his hand. Where was his next port of call going to be? That was my question! This was really getting too close for comfort. You're probably thinking that it was already too close for comfort, right? I bet that you wouldn't have got yourself into this kind of predicament. Anyway, moving swiftly on just like he did, he then moved his arm again but this time I felt his hand wander my way. Do you want to guess where? Bloody hell! Any idea where? Use your imagination! Do I have to spell this out? Was that a yes? Are you sure?

Then, here we go! It started with him reaching out and blindly scoring a direct hit on my groin area with a rather solid grope. I was really not happy! Should I lash out and run? Would I be able to get myself and my rucksack out intact? Do I beckon over an unsuspecting sheep into the cab to distract him? Would he be able to tell the difference? So many questions and thoughts running through my head and all the while, his hand was grappling with my manhood. What should I do?

Instinctively, I pushed his hand away calmly and politely asked him to stop what he was doing, like one does at times like this. To my complete amazement and relief, he stopped and apologised. Yep, you heard right – he bloody apologised! To say that I was relieved was an understatement. Throughout this whole episode, I was in a complete state of panic. On the outside, I was as cool as a cucumber but on the inside, it was a totally different story. How on earth did I get myself into this situation, was the question that was asked countless times by friends. It was good question that I couldn't really answer. Apart from pure stupidity, I don't really have an answer.

Once Dimitri apologised, he climbed out of the cab's bed and sat at the steering wheel. I quickly got myself out and sat in the passenger seat and not a word was said. It was eerily quiet. We sat there in the dark for a long time. Understandably, it was very awkward. He cranked up the lorry's engine and eventually asked me if I was OK. I replied by saying, "Yes, no problem", and that was that. However, I was still on high alert, especially after having my nadgers moulded and manipulated like pieces of putty.

Panic mode hit once more when he stopped again, but this time it was on the side of the motorway and not in a layby. He told me that this is where I had to get out as he was turning off to go to Yugoslavia. He'd never told me that! He said he was going all the way to Thessaloniki! In his mind, he was probably thinking that he was going to go all the way to the promised land, so to speak. Still, I wasn't going to argue; I was happy to get out! I climbed out with my rucksack, munitions bag and my anal virginity intact, which I was more than happy with.

It reminded me of a situation my brother's friend got himself into. Apparently, he got himself smashed at a party and he passed out. The following morning he woke up with a bloke lying next to him. Not only did he have a huge headache but to add insult to injury (I absolutely love that term) his jeans were down by his knees. I'll let you do the maths on that one. Needless to say, he was shocked and not a happy little party goer!

So now we're back to the motorway. I watched the potential fun wagon drive off until his red tail lights vanished. In the words of Rick in *The Young Ones*, I shouted out, "You complete and utter bastard!" into the dark void. In one way, I was thankful that I was away from that situation but now I had another problem. It was around 9.30pm and it was pitch black apart from the occasional lights of passing vehicles, which lit up my path. I was in the middle of nowhere, and ironically, I started singing The Beatles song *Nowhere Man* to myself. I strapped my rucksack on and hung my munitions bag around my neck. I didn't know what I was going to get myself into next, so I took out my torch and Swiss Army knife. I pulled out the blade. This was really something I would not ordinarily do but this was more of a preventative and protective measure. I just didn't know what was out there in terms of wildlife. Were there any hungry wolves and bears out there? I just didn't know. Or even worse... were there humans out there?

I was thinking all this as I walked along the hard shoulder of the motorway. Was it feasible to sleep rough tonight and carry on in daylight? I had no food and no water. There was nothing in sight. There wasn't even a distant flicker of static building lights; just a blanket of darkness. Even the moon wasn't coming out to play to light up the sky. The question was... did I want another lift? Was I ready for another lift? I congratulated myself regarding that question. Was I beginning to think in a sensible way? I probably wasn't! To scarily cap it all, I was actually talking to myself – how bizarre was that? I had to take that risk. I needed a lift. Surely it couldn't happen again... could it?

As I was walking with a torch in one hand and my Swiss Army knife in the other, I began wondering whether the Aussies had made it to the youth hostel. I was pretty sure the French girls and the German couple made it safely. They were the sensible ones... unlike me! So, as all these thoughts were going through my head and without any warning, a lorry slowed and stopped a little way ahead of me. What do I do now? That was the question I was asking myself. I carried on walking towards the lorry, when this guy hung his head out of the window and asked in broken English where I was going. Of all the languages, why English? Anyway, I told him that I was going to Thessaloniki. He replied by saying that he was going into the city and he could drop me off.

I threw caution to the wind, pushed the blade back in and put it into my bag and got in. There was no passenger seat just a couple of sacks containing something or other but it was fine. This guy was quite chatty; a complete contrast to the moustached groin grabber. I noticed immediately that he had a long moustache (what was it with moustaches and truck drivers that day?) a beard, long hair covered by a tatty red baseball cap and DIY tattoos all over his arms. I felt that this guy was decent, as he spoke about his wife and children living in Bulgaria. He said that he loved driving but had spent a lot of time away from his family, delivering goods.

He asked me how I'd ended up walking along the motorway. I told him what had happened and he started laughing that knowing laugh. He said that I was very lucky and that he had heard of some horror stories. These stories also included some truck drivers being on the receiving end as well. He probably meant that drivers had been physically abused. I completely agreed with him in that I was very lucky. I decided that once I got settled, I would ring my mum just to let her know where I was, that I was well and everything was fine. I was always aware why she would worry but this little episode really brought it home to me.

THESSALONIKI

Not long after we entered the outskirts of Thessaloniki, I was dropped off on the roadside. I said goodbye to the driver and he said good luck as if he really meant it! Funny, that! Now, I didn't have a Scooby where I was but I did have the address of the IYH, which was handy.

After asking a few people, I was told that I wasn't too far from the hostel. After buying some water, which I really needed, I found the youth hostel, only to be told that they did not take anyone after 10pm and to come back tomorrow morning at 9am. It was around 11.30pm, so I was metaphorically buggered for the night. Thinking about it, I literally could've been buggered for the night!

I had to find somewhere to stay, even if it was a park bench or a bush. On the surface of it, things seemed to be going from bad to worse and I was quite tired. I felt that I had been running on adrenaline and now it had finally run out. Ahead of me, I saw a large group of people. I naturally wondered what was going on, so I walked towards them (I think most people would have gone in the opposite direction fearing the worst) and it turned out that they had just come out of a cinema. I began to ask if there was a cheap hostel anywhere. Most of the people were pleasant and said they didn't know of hostels as such but there were cheap hotels. Even the cheap hotels would have been too expensive for me. I asked a couple of guys if they knew of anything cheap and cheerful. Instead of recommending somewhere, they actually invited me to stay with them. I said thanks but no thanks and said that I didn't want to put them out. They replied by saying it was no trouble. They wrote down their address and pointed up the road, saying that it was not far from where we were stood. As I politely declined their offer, they said that I was always welcome. Hmmm! It was a lovely gesture but I'd had enough excitement for the day! I carried on walking, looking admiringly at the cakes in the glitzy patisserie shops. Every now and again, I caught the smell of coffee in the air.

Like most places in Europe, there were a huge number of apartment blocks with foyers. The foyers had sofas which looked very inviting. I could feel them beckoning me over to try them out! They would have been perfect for the night. The only problem was that the doors to the buildings housing these wonderful sofas either had a key entry, an intercom and buzzer entry system or a numerical keypad; none of which I could access. I did try random numbers on the keypads quite a few times. Unsurprisingly, I had absolutely no luck. The other option was to try the doors in the hope that one of them had been left ajar or just didn't work properly. Failing that, I kept an eye out for somewhere safe and sheltered to sleep. Well, as safe as it could be I suppose!

It was gone midnight and the tiredness was really making itself known to me. In fact, I was physically and emotionally exhausted. The whole journey from Athens could have gone completely the other way. Like my second truck buddy said, I was very lucky.

Coincidently, speaking of luck, I pushed a door at the entrance to a block and it opened. Caerus, the Greek god of opportunity and luck, definitely had my back. He probably felt sorry for me earlier on. I didn't have to be asked twice, so I very quickly nipped in. An orange leather-cladded sofa was set in a recess which was conveniently out of the way. I thought that this was ideal. I unravelled my sleeping bag and spread it out across the sofa. Very comfortable, I thought. I climbed into my sleeping bag and took my book out to read. The book that I was reading was Jackie Collins' *Hollywood Husbands*, which was fast-moving and such an easy read. It was a bit like reading *The Sun*. Just for your information and my street clout, I don't read *The Sun* newspaper and I never have. I have always found its bias, right-wing leanings and the treatment of the Liverpool 96 very disturbing. If you're unaware what this is about, then please look it up on the internet. In a way, *The Sun* reminds me of George Orwell's book *1984*, where the masses were entertained to keep them oblivious and happy, while political agendas raged on unnoticed. Anyway, I'd found the Jackie Collins book in the hostel in Piraeus, where I did a straight swap with a Mills and Boon book I had finished. I think I marginally got the better deal.

Meanwhile, my sofa was enticing and relaxing me with those big orange eyes... I have to say the foyer was quiet and I was quite comfortable. My eyelids were feeling like lead as I was reading. I must have nodded off because the next thing I knew, there was something wet on my face. Oi! Behave yourselves! Don't even go there! Read on and you'll see what I'm talking about. I woke up startled and realised that I was being sniffed. It was a dog. A bloody big, brown and white St. Bernard! Don't get me wrong, I love dogs but I was momentarily stunned. What was even more disconcerting was the man who accompanied the dog. He was standing behind the dog in all his glory, scantily clad in a dirty white vest and a pair of loose-fitting Y-Fronts. I heard myself say, "Not again!" Did I have a sticker on my forehead saying, "He's up for it today boys. All enquiries welcome!"

What was in the air today? Whatever it was, it felt like it was all heading my way!

The half-clothed man started waving his big hairy arms, saying that I couldn't stay and that I had to leave. I politely argued, saying it was starting to rain, I'd be no trouble and it was only for one night while I waited for the IYH to open. He was having none of it. He insisted that I get out of the building and that he didn't care where I went and if I didn't he would call the Police. He wanted me out. It was fair enough, really. However, he eventually calmed down and said that I could stay in the cupboard, which housed the access to the lift shaft. He showed me the cupboard, saying that it was just for one night and one night only (just like Donna and The Dynamos in Mama Mia the film). I agreed and he went back to his apartment with his dog; it would have been nice if the dog could have stayed with me.

The cupboard had a dim light, which was handy, so I moved everything in. I took the key from the outside and locked the door from the inside. I left the key in the lock, slightly turned, just in case someone had a momentary lapse in humanity. I sat on my sleeping bag taking it all in.

Apart from four beautifully cobwebbed concrete walls, ahead of me was a control panel of some sort (probably a fire alarm) and then more darkness. I shone my torch into the abyss and saw that it was just the back wall of the cupboard with a metal door to the right. I assumed that behind the door was the lift shaft with its resident skeletons. However, I saw something that unnerved me a bit. I noticed that... wait for it... wait for it... there were mousetraps and what I assumed were poisonous mouse or rat pellets sprinkled lovingly on the floor. Great! *Just What I Needed,* to quote a song by The Cars. At this point, beggars couldn't be choosers, so I jumped into my sleeping bag, zipped it up and decided to at least try and get some sleep. I left the light on for a bit of security. I wasn't sure if I was going to get a visit from one of Roland Rat's, or Mickey Mouse's furry relatives.

It was deathly quiet in the cupboard. I'm sure it would have been quite noisy if the lift had kicked in; thankfully it didn't. I was kind of sleeping with my ears on full alert, in case I had any unpleasant surprises. Try to picture the scene. I'm sitting up against the wall in my sleeping bag with my munitions bag lodged between my legs. On top of my sleeping bag was Jackie Collins' smiling face, pitifully looking up at me! To my left was my torch, my opened Swiss Army knife and the cupboard door. To my right was my rucksack, which was all secured, to keep my cute little friends out. On the floor ahead of me were mousetraps, poisonous pellets and what looked like black multi-vitamin pills. I really don't think they were; they were pieces of oval-shaped, rodent shite!

A bit further ahead of me was this hazy darkness, my own personal black hole, my void. I knew that there was nothing there but it's funny how fear takes hold of your imagination and accelerates it 100%. I remember a time when I was about eight or nine years old, around the time of Halloween, when I would hide under my bed sheets (no duvets for us) and I would not come up for air unless I had to. Even then my eyes would be shut so that I wouldn't see any witches flying around on their broomsticks. It really didn't help, having a badly carved out pumpkin that I had made in school, with a lit candle inside casting terrifying shadows on the wall. Why did I have it in my room if I was so frightened, I hear you ask? The simple answer was I wanted to do what all the other kids were doing in my class. I wanted to be part of it all, even though it scared the brown stuff out of me. It was a steep learning curve even at that age. I remember thinking that I was actually scared of this, so why the hell was I doing it? I was questioning social culture and populism even at that age but I didn't realise I was doing it. My mum even said it was not a good idea, but she let me get on with it. Mind you, I would imagine that she was probably mulling over the idea of some kind of disaster involving a fire. To be honest, I didn't know what she was thinking but I'm sure it would have been something like that.

So, as I was saying, I was sat there in the cupboard fully kitted up with hand grenades and an Uzi. I was feeling totally exhausted and was again beginning to nod off with my rat radar fully operational. It was such a quiet environment that you could hear a pin drop. While I was in and out of sleep, I heard footsteps with doors being opened and shut. I assumed that it was the residents with their comings and goings. On one occasion, I heard what I thought was a noise coming from inside the cupboard but I was so tired that I ignored it. I heard the same noise moments later, but this time, I opened my eyes and scanned the cupboard area with my torch. I couldn't really see anything. As I was beginning to nod off again, I heard the same scampering noise. This time I picked up my torch but as I shone it into the darkness, I saw the movement of a small rocking box and that's when reality really hit. I was not alone. There was another resident or residents subletting this one-star rated cupboard. It's a strange thing to say, but as tired and numbly terrified as I was, I felt weirdly at peace with it. It seemed that the tiredness took my mind off my current panic-stricken situation. The time was around 1.30am so I started to read a little bit of Jackie and quickly found I couldn't put it down. The chapters were extremely short and the storyline (if any) was fast-moving. It definitely took my mind off Roland and friends, but not completely.

It was a long night but I did manage to grab some sleep. How much sleep did I have? I really couldn't tell you. For all I knew, there might have been a family of rats on an early morning stroll, with the parents making a comment to their young rattlings. I wouldn't be at all surprised if they pointed me out, saying how the neighbourhood had gone downhill, how dirty I looked and that they would have to get the exterminators in. Can you imagine that happening in another dimension? The thought of it made me chuckle.

I have to say that the whole Roland and Jackie episode took my mind off toilet duties. Speaking of which, it was around 7.30am when I decided to pack up and move out of my evening's lodgings to find a toilet, or a strategically positioned, out-of-sight bush. As I opened the cupboard door, the sun was trying to weakly shine into the foyer without much success. I moved out of the cupboard, switched the light off and bade a fond farewell to Roland and the dark void. I then walked out of the building with all my belongings. The area looked different in the day...

not so daunting. It's always worse turning up somewhere new in the dark.

Some patisseries were open and once again, I could smell the coffee. I desperately needed a coffee and a toilet but not necessarily in that order! I soon came across a patisserie with seats. I bought myself a coffee and croissant, which were reasonably priced. I sat down at the table, taking a few sips of coffee. A couple of the older staff looked at me rather suspiciously. You couldn't really blame them for that. If a rough-looking bloke turns up sits in your establishment (if you had one that is) what would you think? Would you be protective? Once I'd finished consuming the croissant and coffee, I rather sheepishly asked one of the staff members if I could use the toilet. The lady that I asked said that there were no toilets. I said I'd seen the toilet sign and that I had just bought a coffee and a croissant. So, in effect, I was paying to use the toilet as a customer. I might have looked rough but I was a paying punter, so to speak! I'm talking about food and drink here just in case some of your minds have wandered into an alternative punter realm!

Anyway, she falsely smiled and allowed me to use it. I asked her to keep an eye on my rucksack which she did and I proceeded to take the route in a cross-legged manner to the toilet. The toilet was large and clean with pleasant smelling odours. Actually, I could have spent the night in there; at least I would have had my own en-suite. Once I had naturally lost a few hundred grams, I took out my toothbrush and soap, that earlier I had put in my bag and had a well-deserved wash. I wiped any water off the floor and left the toilet as I found it, ready for the next person. I was pleased with that. There's nothing worse than not cleaning up after you've used something.

I picked up my rucksack, said thank-you in Greek and casually walked out. As I walked out, I saw one of the ladies from behind the counter rush at break-neck towards the toilet. She'd either had a sudden and unexpected bout of bowel movement, or she was checking to see if I'd caused any damage. It was probably the latter! People are so territorial, but I would probably do the same given what I looked like. I would have been a bit more subtle about it, though.

I decided that once I was booked into the hostel, I was going to do nothing else but sleep. It had been a long thirty odd hours. Little did I know that those thirty odd hours were going to be further extended. The road that I'd walked down the previous night seemed so different this morning. I'd even go as far to say that it was quite pleasant. The sun was trying to break through the clouds again with some success, throwing spears of light onto the ground. I quite liked the earthy look of this part of Thessaloniki.

I eventually found the hostel, which seemed like it had been in the wars. Why did all these IYH hostels look like they had seen better days? Anyway I was a tad early, so I took my rucksack off, sat on the steps looking at the building itself and wondered if the others had booked in. It really did need a lick of fresh paint and plastering here and there. I could see myself staying in Thessaloniki a while. I had been told that the coastline and surrounding areas were beautiful and lush. I wondered if the hostel needed a general dogsbody in return for lodging and breakfast. That would be ideal. My thoughts drifted to the others again. Had they booked into the hostel? Was there any room? Let's wait and see.

My daydream was interrupted by what sounded like a prison officer in Ronnie Barker's *Porridge* unlocking the main doors. The doors were opened and I was up those steps like a ferret up a drainpipe! I absolutely adore that simile. Imagine teaching that simile to primary school children. I wonder if children even know what a ferret is, let alone what that particular simile means... no offence meant. It would have to be a whole new lesson dedicated to the characteristics and habitats of ferrets. It would obviously have to be an ad-hoc, one-off type of curriculum lesson.

Just for your information, coal miners in Yorkshire apparently used to put live ferrets down their trousers. Are your eyes watering yet? Mine certainly are! Who in their right mind would want to that? This was a popular competitive hobby. The winner would be the one who would release the ferret last. It was also known as 'ferret-legging'. It's believed to have originated during the time when only the wealthy were allowed to keep ferrets for hunting. Animal poachers would keep their illegal ferrets in their trousers to avoid being found out by the gamekeepers. Either way, it would be a painful outcome! I'm not sure which option I would prefer... being caught by the gamekeeper, which would end up with a harsh punishment or having a psychotic ferret down one's trousers and having one's nadgers used to sharpen his or her teeth on. Then there's the claws; let's not forget them! Thinking about it, I'm going to have to stick to snakes. I have one of my own you know; they're no trouble! You don't even have to feed them. All you need to do is take them on an outing about two or three times a day. They're happy with that; unlike ferrets.

Now I've finished explaining the antics of ferrets, something that I wouldn't have normally written about, I booked into the hostel and was shown to a dormitory, which had four metal-framed bunk beds. I was basically told that I could take any bunk which did not have a bag on it. There were six unoccupied beds, so I took one of the bottom bunks next to a window. I then I recognised two rucksacks on two of the beds that belonged to the Aussies. They had badges sewn on showing which countries they had been to. I was glad they'd made it. That was good, so I decided to catch up with them later. As for the others, I wasn't sure.

Now that I was in, I decided to have a snooze. I unstrapped and unrolled my sleeping bag, let out the ferrets and laid it on the sheet-less mattress. The room was a bit smelly but it was fine. I've had worse. As I closed my eyes, the receptionist came in and said that the hostel was closed daily from 10am until 1pm for cleaning, and apologised for not mentioning it earlier. To be honest, and as tired as I was, I was surprisingly okay with it. I picked myself up, took my munitions bag and walked down the stairs. As I walked downstairs, I could hear an American women's rather irate voice, saying that she had just checked in and all she wanted to do was to sleep. Looks like we both had the same idea but it was not going to happen for a few hours.

I stood next to her and chipped in saying that I had slept rough last night. I added that all I wanted to do was exactly what she wanted to do, and that was to sleep. She turned to me, scanned me up and down and turned back to the poor receptionist and carried on with what she was saying. The reply she got was the same as mine, "I'm sorry but we clean the hostel between 10am and 1pm". After she reluctantly accepted what was said, she was shown to her room where she left her rucksack.

I hung around outside sitting on the steps looking at a map of Thessaloniki that I had acquired from the hostel. The American girl came and sat next to me and apologised if she came over as rude. Her excuse was that she was stressed and tired. She introduced herself as Joni (as in Joni Mitchell, the singer) and said that she had been on a coach from Paris and was very tired. She was slim, around my height, which wasn't very tall, had long straight blonde hair which I have to say needed a wash! She spoke in what I can only describe as a New York accent. You never can tell (which incidentally is a great Chuck Berry song), but I'm happy to say that my first impressions were right; she was a New Yorker!

I started quietly whistling the intro to Frank Sinatra's *New York, New York*, and Joni piped in with the opening line, *Start spreading the news, I'm leaving today...* We both had a good giggle about that. I asked her if she was from New York and she said that I'd guessed correctly. We sat around talking about where we had been and where we were heading. I said that for me, it depended very much on the wind as to where I was heading. Joni, on the other hand, had a much more solid itinerary, which was to stay in Thessaloniki for a few days, make her way to Athens and then catch a ferry to Alexandria on the North Coast of Egypt. Now, Egypt was a place I wanted to visit. It was definitely on my list of places to potter about in, which I eventually did.

I looked at Joni's hair and implied that it would be a good idea to dye her hair another colour before she left Greece. She was already aware of the possible problems, and said she had invested in a pack of dark brown Henna hair dye. Joni went on to say that she would also wear a headscarf. She seemed very streetwise and I saw that side of her come out more and more as time went on.

We decided to hang out together and started to walk in no particular direction. We chatted away the whole time, which was great. It certainly kept me awake. Like I said, it was a very long day and night! We came across what I can only describe as a pedestrianised area which was on a slight hill. We took our lives into our hands and ran across the busy road where no one stops and where everyone hoots their horns (very much like Athens) and only asks you questions after they've run you down. It's rather exaggerated but that's how it seemed. Once we were across the road, the area seemed busy but at the same time it was quiet in terms of noise. The atmosphere was pleasant and very relaxed. It was weird. Behind us was the hustle and bustle, the honking of horns accompanied by the customary Greek drivers' insults and ahead of us was peace. A little bit of tranquillity surrounded by chaos.

This pedestrianised area crossed other busy main roads and carried on up the hill. We carried on walking and chatting and we both mentioned that we were hungry. We both didn't want to spend too much money on food or anything else. I was always careful with my money and I felt happy with the amount I had left. I wasn't sure what Joni's budget was like. Anyhow, we sat and shared a sandwich on a central wall when we noticed a bit of a commotion going on a bit further up. As we listened, we heard some people shouting in broken English and the word 'malaka', which was quite often thrown in for good measure. So like any other upstanding and nosy human beings, we jumped off the wall and walked rather quickly (not far short of running so we wouldn't miss anything) to where the action was. As we approached, we heard an American accent which

Joni pointed out was a redneck accent. The funny thing was that I recognised the voice. I mentioned it to Joni, who didn't quite believe me. I couldn't quite place the voice and then it dawned on me... it was Jake! I pushed to the front, closely followed by my newly acquired buddy. Jake was on his own, in the middle of the little square with his camping gas stove, making himself what smelt like coffee. The locals were basically saying that he wasn't allowed to use a gas stove in a public place and he was replying with his standard stock phase that they were all communists. Joni's reaction was one of embarrassment on behalf of the American people. She actually said to me not to acknowledge him as the crowd might even turn on us. I have to say she was right.

The whole situation was escalating to the point of some harsh language being used on both sides. Someone had obviously called the police, as armed officers turned up. You don't mess with the police in Greece. One thing I did know about the Greek police is that they would clobber you first and ask you questions afterwards. The questioning would occur after one's arms had been fractured, accompanied with blood dripping from one's forehead and a chicken gyros delicately shoved up one's rear orifice. However, if you were civil, I would assume you would be OK.

Unfortunately, Jake called the police officers who attended the scene 'communists', when they politely asked him to switch off the stove and move on. That was not a good move as he found out! One of the officers who I might add wasn't exactly petite, pushed Jake over and put the gas stove out. Jake protested and again called them all communists, which in all honesty didn't go down very well and the rest was history. He was hit across the arms and legs with what looked like a wooden baton and was carted off into a waiting police car. All the while, he was shouting out some quite amusingly descriptive obscenities. I'll leave the detail to your imagination! He even shouted out, "I'm an American citizen. You can't do this!" What a stupid thing to say... as if it gives him the authority to verbally abuse people and flout their rules. The crowd that had gathered all cheered as he was pretty much thrown like a rag doll into the back of the police car. While all this was happening, the crowd were shouting, "Malaka! Malaka! Malaka!" I have no idea what happened to him after that. I never saw him again. If that happened in this day and age, I would guarantee you that there would be an army of mobile phone camera warriors recording it all and posting it on their respective social media feeds. Thankfully, the technology wasn't around. Things were so much more straightforward then.

After all the excitement had died down, I explained who Jake was and where our paths had crossed. As we carried on walking further up the hill, we came across a square with an old church in the middle of it. We walked through the square to the other side and carried on aimlessly through what looked like a residential area, which was nestled at the base of the hill that we were heading towards. Foolishly, we thought it would be a good idea to go to the top of the hill to see what the view was like over the city. We probably made it halfway up, when we both said how tired we were. Like I said, I'd had quite an eventful thirty something hours to say the least and Joni had been on one of those coach journeys that never seems to end. As Joni said, the lack of sleep is bought along with the ticket!

We sat under a tree and seeing that we'd come this far, we decided to carry on up the hill. By this point we were thirsty as we had drunk our last drop of water. To add to it, we were hungry but we carried on like Spartan warriors, so to speak! As I read this back to myself, it seemed as if I was watching a film about an aeroplane crashing in the desert and that the survivors had become very desperate as they had drunk their last droplets of water. That was us but without the aeroplane crash and the desert!

Anyway, we walked a little further and we heard lots of voices and laughing coming from somewhere ahead of us. As we followed our ears and dragged ourselves up the hill, we came across a road. Across the road we saw a remote restaurant which was accompanied by the same jollity we'd heard earlier. We rushed stealthily across the road and sat behind a low stone wall which was part of the restaurant's perimeter. We were sat with our backs to the outside wall wondering what to do next. We were thirsty and hungry. We peered over the wall like two soldiers assessing the situation and saw a handful of people including children, eating and generally having fun. We assumed it was a couple of families having lunch. There was no way we were going to be able to afford restaurant food. So, with that said, we decided that the only option was to go back down the hill into the residential area and find ourselves some cheaper food and drink.

We stood up ready to move on when I noticed that they were leaving. I sat straight back down and pulled Joni down with me. I had asked Joni if she had ever eaten leftovers from a friend's plate. She replied that she had. She asked me why I'd asked that question, so I answered that we could the same here. The only difference being was that we didn't know these people, but we could help ourselves to the leftovers on their plates. Without any hesitation, she agreed. So, we waited until they had left the restaurant and we tentatively moved in as if we were on a secret military mission, looking around to make sure that we weren't seen by any staff.

I got to the tables first and saw pieces of pizza, rice, meat, salad, bread etc. along with half full beer and soft drinks bottles. We explored the table of leftover food like butterflies and began grazing on some pieces. I have to say it was delicious! In hindsight, I'm not sure if the food was that delicious as we were both so hungry, or was it because it really was such good food? Probably both... and then thrown into the mix was the fact that we shouldn't be doing what we were doing. With that said, it was probably all three! I really hope all that makes sense!

So, there we were, Joni and I, in the covered garden area with rays of sunlight piercing through the bird-pecked holes in the canopy, coupled with the backdrop of the hills. I have to admit it was a lovely location. Keeping our eyes peeled as Shaw Taylor would say on *Police 5*, we nervously munched away. I watched Joni firmly plant her teeth into a piece of pizza which I had offered her. At that moment, we both stopped and watched two waiters walk towards us. It was evident to the waiters that we were about to run because as they came towards us one of them put his hands out and told us in Greek to wait. I wondered if they were going to call the police or just chase us off with an electrified cattle prod.

As Joni began making for the wall, one of the waiters asked us if we were hungry. Personally, I thought it was a bit of a daft question as he could see us tucking in, but I have to say they were absolutely brilliant. He asked us in Greek and I tried to reply in Greek, which again was a disaster, so I reverted to English. At this point Joni joined in and between us we managed to talk it through. The waiters told us that all the food on the tables would be thrown away. They asked us if we would like the food and drink that had not been half eaten. Joni and I looked at each other and Joni asked if we had to pay. I thought that it was a great question. The waiters laughed, shook their heads and said that it had already been paid for. Now, that was good news. We were ushered to a table. The waiters cleared all the tables and filtered out all the untouched food and drink and lovingly put everything on our table along with cutlery and napkins!

After having to rough it so often, this attention was a bit alien to me but very welcome indeed. It was amazing and so unexpected! As we started munching, the waiters carried on clearing and insisted that there was no need to rush, so we didn't. Although the food was cold, it was still quite tasty.

The earlier anticipation of being caught was quite exciting in a strange sort of way. Mind you, having been caught munching away turned that excitement into terror. We were very appreciative about what had just happened and we thanked our lucky stars that these were good people. And to cap it all they offered us coffee! How fantastic was that? It's only at times like this that you realise that the only things that matter in life are the basic things – shelter, food and drink. I'd probably throw respect in there somewhere as well.

After we had appreciatively finished consuming the leftovers, we started to pile the plates together and generally cleared the table. I was always taught to do that as a child. Clearing the table has stayed with me. Joni had noticed. I started clearing first and she helped out and said that her parents (mainly her mum) always cleared the table, while her younger sister and older brothers just walked away not lifting a finger. They were never taught or encouraged to do chores around their house. It turns out that it was a pretty big house and I got the idea that money in her household wasn't an issue. In saying that, full marks to Joni for trying to save her money and not blow it while travelling. That was one part of her personality that I liked. She didn't take things for granted.

Anyway, I'm kind of going off track again. After we'd tided up and had given the waiters our sincere, heartfelt thanks, a slim, middle-aged lady came out and introduced herself as the owner of the restaurant. She said that she had been watching us from inside the restaurant and was impressed that we tidied up after ourselves. She went on to say that some people treat her waiters and waitresses as if it was their God-given right to look down on them and treat them disrespectfully. She obviously had an issue with that, and she was quite right to do so. We ended up sitting down again and having another coffee and chatting with her for around a good hour. The waiters eventually joined us along with some other staff. It was such a great afternoon. I'd never imagined it would turn out like this. Not in a million years! If I could translate that moment into a song, it would be Depeche Modes', *Just Can't Get Enough*, because these moments are quite rare and you don't want them to end.

We eventually said our goodbyes, not before we were invited back the next day to sample more leftovers and to have more chats, which was nice. We didn't go back the next day but we turned up a couple of days later, with a small box of Greek pastries as a thank you. We were once again fed more leftovers, had more chats and coffees and of course, we all had pieces of the pastries that we had bought them. It was a bit like the bag of grapes syndrome when you're visiting someone in hospital. You end up eating the grapes.

Anyway, back to the moment, as we left, the owner gave us a bottle of water, a can of Pepsi and a couple of food parcels to take away. It was as if we were the two remaining descendants of Klondike Pete and that we had found golden nuggets in the hills. Look up this fictional character if you don't know who he is. That's how it felt. It was just wonderful; such good people. It was a lovely gesture.

We took a slow walk down to the seafront and spent the rest of the day and early evening hanging out along that stretch. There was lots of talking and laughing. We were OK for food and drink as the restaurant had sorted us out. It's a good feeling when you haven't got to be anywhere or do anything in particular. It was yet more confirmation as to why I was away from the UK. I didn't have to conform to the whims of others around me. I just did what I wanted to do and hung out with who I wanted to hang out with. I knew that I had made the right decision to travel on my own. I could afford to be totally selfish. I mean that in a good way. I could please myself on all fronts and not offend anyone. I had no one to answer to. There was no dogma and I didn't have to adhere to other people's needs and fears. It was just me and no one else. I had this conversation with Joni and she completely agreed with that line of thought. She added that everyone should experience travelling in this way, as it gives you the space to think without external pressures. Although she hadn't been away that long, she was beginning to realise it and these conversations over the next few days helped her.

We had quite a long chat about it and we spoke about people we knew who would benefit from this kind of travelling. We both came to the conclusion that we were beginning to see how people lived and survived and that we were grateful for what we had! It was also the luck of the draw as to where and what you were born into. These things were becoming very apparent to me as time went on; the inequalities of life! Most people have to work harder to change their lives, if indeed they want to, or are able to, or have the skills to. There are those, however, who don't see it or can't see because they are so far removed from it! That's why Eddie and the Hot Rods' song *Do Anything You Wanna Do* is so important to me. Even now it remains topical! The lyrics are spot on! Timeless! I wanted to print the lyrics here but the publishing company wanted a fee and asked a million and one questions, all of which I didn't have the answers for. So instead, I suggest you

Google the lyrics and hopefully you might see what I'm wittering on about!

I was having such a good time that it didn't register how tired I was, until we got back to the hostel. The second I put my head down that was it! I went out like a light and slept without even realising I had fallen asleep, only to be woken up by the Aussies. It was great to see them. Unlike me, they had had no problems on their journeys to Thessaloniki. I told them what happened and they just fell about the place laughing. I asked about the others and they hadn't seen them at all. I suppose we all have the right to change our plans and minds. The Aussies had decided to catch a train to Istanbul in a few hours. Once again, we said our goodbyes. Up until that point, I had slept really well.

I had arranged to meet Joni outside on the steps of the hostel around 9.30ish the following day. The hostel was clean and the toilets were remarkably okay, to say that people had used them that morning. Mind you, it only takes one messy bugger to spoil it for everyone else!

I made my way outside and saw Joni lounging on the steps looking at a map. She was probably planning what we were going do. Like the day before, I began singing the chorus of a song. This time it was Gerrard

Kenny's *New York, New York.* As I finished the line, *'New York, New York, So good they named it twice'*, she replied, *'New York, New York, All the scandal and the vice'*. I remember thinking how amazed I was that she even knew the song! It was a funny moment. We carried on from where we left off the night before; we were having fun!

Having decided that we needed some breakfast, we bought one coffee and one croissant and shared it. We thought it would be a good idea to hitch a ride to a place on the coast just south of Thessaloniki called Kallikratia. If translated, Kallikratia would mean good government. 'Kalli' means good and 'kratia' means government/rule. This is just a piece of useless information for you to ponder on.

We managed to hitch a ride with a good natured and very chatty couple. Joni mentioned that I was Greek but pointed out that my command of the Greek language was pretty rubbish and that's coming from an American! This was the result of yesterday's piss taking from the restaurant owner, in which Joni gleefully took part. Our hosts wholeheartedly agreed! They said that it sounded like Greek but it was hard to follow. I could see that Joni was trying not to break out into a fit of girlie giggles while saying, "He tries his best!" and "I wouldn't want him to give me directions in Greek!" It was funny and the lovely thing about it was the fact that the couple joined in with her. It was great for us because by the time we settled into the journey, we were already there. It was around a forty-five minute journey. They pointed us in the right direction towards the seafront and we bought another coffee and croissant and shared it again.

I suppose it was like any other place really. It was quaint, relatively quiet and a complete contrast to Thessaloniki's energy. It was very a welcome change. We spent the day walking along the beach, barefooted, and generally having a laugh. At one point Joni started singing lyrics to a song which I recognised and sang along with her. The song was called *Remember Walking in The Sand* which was quite apt, as we were so obviously walking in the sand! I asked her where she had heard the song and she said that it was an Aerosmith song. I replied by saying that it was a sixties song by The Shangri-Las and that my brother had it on one of those K-Tel compilation albums! It was funny as she was adamant that it was an Aerosmith song and I was saying that it wasn't.

This was similar to a conversation I'd had with Lisa about Catholics and Christians. Lisa was saying that Catholics were not Christians and I was saying that they were. Even to this day we have a good laugh about it.

Anyway, in the end, Joni and I exchanged addresses and decided to write to each other regarding the nature of the song and other things. It turns out that in her first letter she acknowledged that Aerosmith didn't actually write the song and that they had covered it. These days we would just look up the information on our phones and get instant gratification, instead of waiting months and months to get home and write to each other to find out. As a result, we had quite a good discussion about music. We had a similar taste in music in that we both liked bands like the Ramones, Blondie etc. It was yet another great feeling of having no responsibilities and doing exactly what I wanted to do. I was constantly thinking that I was presently living a wonderful life; doing what I wanted to do! I can't really express how excited and content I felt during these times. There's a great song by Elvis Presley called *What A Wonderful Life* which, I would say, sums up how I felt at the time and still do to this day. In these days of technology, take the time to look it up, have a listen and follow the lyrics. The title of this book, *No Boss, No Hassle, No Plan* is actually inspired by this song. Both Eddie and the Hot Rods' *Do Anything You Wanna Do* and Elvis Presley's *What A*

Wonderful Life are hugely inspirational for me in terms of life and how we go about it.

The day moved on quite quickly and we sat on the beach watching the sunset and all its amazing colours and images. While we watched the sunset, we communally munched on a shared gyro. Unfortunately, there were no freebies this time!

I have to say that it was another good day; most enjoyable! It was dark and the nights were starting to get a bit chilly. We eventually managed to hitch a ride back but the ride back was not as lively as the ride out. Still, the main thing is that we had a ride back!

Joni was great fun! She had a wicked and sharp sense of humour which complemented my own, but like all good things, it was time to move on. After a few more days of pottering, we went our separate ways. Joni bought a train ticket to Athens with the view of getting a ferry to Alexandria in Egypt and I wasn't sure what I was going do. Nothing new there, I hear you mutter. Again, it was sad saying goodbye to someone that I got on well with but this was the nature of what I was doing. I did not want to get too settled with people and with places. I was just into enjoying the moment and exploring myself. That to me was and still is very important.

I eventually made the decision to venture into Macedonia, which at the time was part of the former Yugoslavia. It was formed in 1918, after World War 1. Yugoslavia was occupied in 1941 during World War 2 by the Axis Powers which were Germany, Italy and Hungary. Yugoslavia comprised of Bosnia and Herzegovina, Croatia, Macedonia, Montenegro, Serbia and Slovenia. My destination was the IYH in the city of Skopje. If you get time, read up about the history of the former Yugoslavia. It's very interesting.

So, this is where I will stop for now. It's to be continued in a second book. I hope you've enjoyed this six-week snapshot so far.

Until the next time...

www.ingramcontent.com/pod-product-compliance
Ingram Content Group UK Ltd.
Pitfield, Milton Keynes, MK11 3LW, UK
UKHW041958260225
455621UK00001B/1